W9-BSX-911

Death

Central Problems of Philosophy
Series Editor: John Shand

This series of books presents concise, clear, and rigorous analyses of the core problems that preoccupy philosophers across all approaches to the discipline. Each book encapsulates the essential arguments and debates, providing an authoritative guide to the subject while also introducing original perspectives. This series of books by an international team of authors aims to cover those fundamental topics that, taken together, constitute the full breadth of philosophy.

Published titles

Action
Rowland Stout

Causation and Explanation
Stathis Psillos

Death
Geoffrey Scarre

Free Will
Graham McFee

Knowledge
Michael Welbourne

Meaning
David E. Cooper

Mind and Body
Robert Kirk

Modality
Joseph Melia

Ontology
Dale Jacquette

Paradox
Doris Olin

Perception
Barry Maund

Relativism
Paul O'Grady

Scepticism
Neil Gascoigne

Truth
Pascal Engel

Universals
J. P. Moreland

Forthcoming titles

God
Jay Wood

Realism and Anti-Realism
Stuart Brock & Edwin Mares

Rights
Duncan Ivison

The Self
Stephen Burwood

Value
Derek Matravers

Death

Geoffrey Scarre

Regis College Library
1 MARY STREET
TORONTO ONTARIO, CANADA
M4Y 2R5

WITHDRAWN

McGill-Queen's University Press
Montreal & Kingston • Ithaca

BD
444
S33
2007

© Geoffrey Scarre 2007

ISBN 978-0-7735-3240-3 (bound)
ISBN 978-0-7735-3241-0 (paper)

Legal deposit first quarter 2007
Bibliothèque nationale du Québec

This book is copyright under the Berne Convention.
No reproduction without permission.
All rights reserved.

Published simultaneously outside North America
by Acumen Publishing Limited

McGill-Queen's University Press acknowledges the financial support of
the Government of Canada through the Book Publishing Development
Program (BPIDP) for its activities.

Library and Archives Canada Cataloguing in Publication

Scarre, Geoffrey
    Death / Geoffrey Scarre.

Includes bibliographical references and index.
ISBN 978-0-7735-3240-3 (bound)
ISBN 978-0-7735-3241-0 (pbk.)

1. Death. 2. Life. I. Title.

BD444.S365 2007   128'.5   C2006-906313-3

Excerpt from "Do Not Go Gentle Into That Good Night" in *Collected Poems*
and *The Poems of Dylan Thomas*, © 1952 by Dylan Thomas, reprinted
by permission of J. M. Dent and New Directions Publishing Corp.

Designed and typeset by Kate Williams, Swansea.
Printed and bound by Cromwell Press, Trowbridge.

Contents

Acknowledgements

I am particularly grateful to Steven Luper and Anthony Bash for invaluable comments on an earlier draft of this book, and to colleagues and students in the Philosophy Department at the University of Durham with whom I have been discussing the topic of death (not too depressingly, I hope) for many years. John Shand gave me generous advice and encouragement at the outset of this project, and Steven Gerrard at Acumen has been a kind and understanding editor throughout. I am also greatly indebted to the sharp copy-editing eye of Kate Williams. It is a pleasure to record my thanks to all without whose help this would have been a much poorer book.

Geoffrey Scarre, Durham

1 The nature of death

Death may seem to be a rather morbid subject for philosophical speculation. Why, after all, should the living concern themselves with a state that, by definition, they do not occupy? Death – the sickle-wielding reaper, the biblical king of terrors – has not yet arrived for any reader of these lines. In one of the most famous reflections on death, the Greek philosopher Epicurus reminds us that "so long as we exist, death is not with us; but when death comes, then we do not exist". Epicurus concludes from this that death is of no concern to either the living or the dead, "since for the former it is not, and the latter are no more" (Epicurus 1926: 85).

Still, as many philosophers have willingly or unwillingly conceded, it is hard to cultivate a state of genuine indifference to the fact that we will all eventually die. The thought that the people we love will die, whether before or after us, is inevitably painful. And it is hard to reconcile ourselves to the knowledge that we ourselves will finally shuffle off this mortal coil. Whatever else death may be, my dying marks the end of all those activities, projects, relationships and commitments that give sense and distinctiveness to my life. This termination of what I care about can scarcely be insignificant to me (or to others, with whose lives my own has interlocked). As Mary Mothersill succinctly puts it, "death is the deadline for all my assignments" (1987: 90).[1] Any unfinished business I have at that point will remain unfinished (by me, at least). Even if I should be fortunate enough to die painlessly, my death will deprive me of whatever gives value to my life, including the opportunity to pursue a range of rewarding and hitherto untried possibilities. Of course, it will also relieve me of those evils that afflict my existence, although unless I have had an outstandingly bad life with little hope of improvement, death is likely to make a net negative impact on my existential balance sheet. Death is the end of the script with no hope of a sequel, unless (which I shall argue is unlikely) there exists some form of afterlife.

But here, as Epicureans point out, there is a puzzle. For while it is natural to speak of my death as depriving *me* of actual and potential sources of satisfaction, to anyone who believes that death is extinction of the self, there is henceforth no *me* to suffer any loss. Death is the end not only of the play but of the actor. Yet if the fundamental loss involved in death is the loss of myself, can death really be an evil, or are the Epicureans right to hold that, as a condition without a subject, it is a thing indifferent?

Whether Epicurus's view that death is "nothing to us" represents a profound insight or a subtle sophistry is a matter we shall return to. It is just one of the many problems concerning the nature of death and the ethical issues surrounding it that we shall be addressing in the course of this study. However, Epicurus is obviously right to say that while we are alive, death is not with us. And it is this trite remark that may make us wonder whether it is not morbid and superfluous to be exercising our minds on thoughts of death. Jesus's advice to let the dead bury their dead (Matthew 8:22) might be construed as a metaphorical mode of making much the same point. Nevertheless, although it would be unwise to become obsessed with death, and to allow thoughts of our impending end to poison our daily existence, there is one – very far from morbid – reason for not retreating to the opposite extreme and doing our best to squeeze death out of our consciousness. This is that reflecting on death and its significance doubles as an illuminating way of reflecting on life.

Any sense of paradox about this claim is soon dispelled. There is a well-known story about Dr Samuel Johnson rebutting the suggestion that he had penned an eloquent appeal on behalf of a clergyman facing a capital sentence for fraud. "Depend upon it, sir," retorted the great lexicographer, "when a man knows he is to be hanged in a fortnight, it concentrates his mind wonderfully" (Boswell 1949: vol. 2, 123).[2] In a similar way but on a (hopefully) longer time scale, our awareness that our own days are numbered can help to focus our attention on making our lives maximally rich and rewarding.

The Roman Stoic philosopher Seneca is just one of many writers to have warned against wasting the limited time we have. Those who squander time as though they had an infinite supply of it in reserve are fools, says Seneca, since they make poor use of "the one thing in which it is right to be stingy" (2005: 61). People who do not think about their own frailty or notice how time is passing are shocked, when death comes, to realize how little has been done. It is not surprising that they find death frightening: "Old age overtakes them when they are still mentally childish, and they face it unprepared and unarmed" (*ibid.*: 69). For those, by contrast, who spend their time wisely in the knowledge it is a finite commodity, "life is long enough" (*ibid.*: 59).

To recast Seneca's insight in the language of existentialist philosophy, a life that meanders without any firm sense of direction, being frittered away on frivolous pursuits, is a life lacking in authenticity (a word deriving from the Greek *authentes*, meaning someone who does things for himself). Decisions are made on the basis of whim or custom rather than serious reflection about priorities. Inauthentic people tend to do what is expected of them, allowing their course to be dictated by others or by circumstances and taking little trouble to design their own lives in the light of their own appraisal of the constraints and opportunities. Having limited horizons and being reluctant to dwell on ultimate questions, they are controlled by their fate rather than controlling it. If they think at all about the long term, their ideas are generally conventional and conformist. Death, like other events, tends to take them unawares.[3] François Duc de La Rochefoucauld observed that "Few people are well-acquainted with death. It is generally submitted to through stupor and custom, not resolution: most men die merely because they cannot help it" (1786: 27). It is sobering to note that the duke apparently believed such inauthenticity to be the normal human condition.

This book will, then, be at least as much about life as about death. Thinking about death should help us to identify the conditions for authentic living. If this seems a somewhat pretentious assertion, I should immediately add that I make no claim in this work to provide final answers to any of the questions that I shall raise. Philosophers often express more confidence in their ability to locate important questions than in their capacity to answer them.

This is not just false modesty on their part (and indeed, philosophers are not especially noted for humility). It stems from a recognition that many of the questions that philosophers tackle are not only hard but also are not suitably provided with once-and-for-all answers, being rather perennial foci of attention for thoughtful men and women. The reason why philosophers are still asking very similar questions about the nature of goodness, truth or beauty to those posed by Plato is not that no one has been clever enough in the intervening two and a half millennia to come up with the answers, but that the issues they raise need to be addressed afresh by the members of any society that considers itself civilized. And so it is with issues of life and death. It is important to ask the questions even though we know that any answers we arrive at will only be interim and provisional (and that some of the questions may defeat us entirely).

But first we must become clearer about what death *is*. If we are to discuss existentially significant and metaphysically taxing problems about death and its relation to life, we need as a preliminary to know what we are talking about. And this may seem a fairly easy task. Can we not just define death as the absence of life? It is not usually too difficult to distinguish a corpse from a living person and we can always call on medical technology in cases that are doubtful. But when we do philosophy, little is as simple as it initially appears. Neither explaining precisely our concept of death nor determining the criteria for saying that someone is dead is as straightforward as we might have expected.

Here are a few of the problems. We may say that the dead lack life, but then we need to say what we mean by "life". Many people, for religious or philosophical reasons (or from sheer wishful thinking), believe that bodily death is not the end of us and that we continue to exist as subjects of an afterlife of some kind. Does this amount to saying that we are not really dead but have merely changed our dwelling place? It certainly indicates that we may be begging a (literally) vital question if we propose to define death as the extinction of the person. Moreover, those who believe that human beings survive the demise of the body but that animals and plants finish when their physical functions cease are working with a dual concept of death, according to which death is extinction in the subhuman categories only.

Even if we shelve questions about an afterlife, there are difficulties – which are becoming increasingly familiar in medical and legal contexts – in deciding at what point of physical decline a person is dead. Should we say that a person is dead when the heart and lungs have ceased to function (i.e. where there is cessation of heartbeat and breathing), or should we look to brain-death as the crucial criterion? Neither of these proposals, as we shall see, is beyond objection, particularly nowadays when so-called "life-support" mechanisms are available to sustain vital functions long beyond the stage at which the subject's own organs have become incapable of doing so.

Some philosophers, too, have pondered the implications of cryogenic and other potential techniques for preserving bodies intact after death in the hope that medical advances will one day produce a cure for whatever fatal condition carried off their owners. If Wilbur should thus be given a new lease of life a century after his body was deep frozen, should we say that Wilbur has been resurrected from the dead or that (unlike Wilfrid, who expired from the same cause but whose body was allowed to decay) he had never really died?

The rest of this chapter will be devoted to exploring some of these issues in more detail.

The definition of death

Let us start with the problems involved in saying exactly what death is. It is helpful, to begin with, to distinguish between the notions of dying, death and being dead. These may be conveniently characterized as, respectively, a process, an event and a state. However, the term "death" is often used to denote all three of these, and we should be alert to this ambiguity, although context usually makes it plain which the word is referring to. Just occasionally it can be problematic, as when a writer talks about the "fear of death" and it is unclear whether this means fear of the process, the event or the state. Nowadays, when most deaths, at least in richer countries, are relatively painless, thanks to the medical help and succour that is available to the dying, the process and event have lost some (though by no means all) of their traditional horror. In his introduction to Michel de Montaigne's essay "To Philosophize is to Learn How to Die" (1987: 89), M. A. Screech reminds us that in days when the close of life was for many an excruciating experience, fear of dying and of death was more acute and widespread than it is now. We therefore need to be careful, when reading older authors who speak about the fear of death, not to assume too readily that they are referring, as we are more likely to be doing when we use the phrase, to the *state* of being dead.

It is very doubtful whether it is possible to arrive at a single and univocal definition of death that will accord with our intuitions in all circumstances. It is true that there are often no difficulties in recognizing that a person is dead. When the butler discovers a corpse in the library with a knife through its heart, he has no qualms about calling in the police to investigate a murder. But not all cases are so simple.

To begin to see why, consider for example the definition of death proposed by the US President's Commission for the Study of Ethical Problems in Medicine and Biomedical and Behavioral Research, set up by Ronald Reagan in 1981. This proposal, which for a while found widespread acceptance in the US, runs as follows: "An individual who has sustained either (1) irreversible cessation of circulatory and respiratory functions, or (2) irreversible cessation of all functions of the entire brain, including the brain stem, is dead" (quoted in Leming & Dickinson 2002: 43). It is sometimes asked, and with reason, whether clause (1) of this disjunctive definition states an adequate sufficient condition for saying that someone is dead. When breathing and heartbeat stop, the brain will be starved of oxygen and die within a few minutes. But in the interval between the former and the latter event would we wish to say that the subject was dead, or only dying? Even where a post-mortem examination subsequently reveals that the cessation of circulatory and respiratory functions could not have been reversed by the most sophisticated medical technology, many of us might prefer to say not that the subject died at this point but that his death then became inevitable. Additionally, devotees of science fiction, including the thought experiments of philosophers, may like to ponder the implications of removing a brain from a dying body and keeping it alive in a vat. If such an operation were to be performed, then provided that the mental life of the brain suffered no radical disruption (in particular, where there was no serious discontinuity of memory), we would probably wish to say that the subject remained alive, despite the cessation of anything resembling ordinary processes of respiration or blood circulation.

In the last few years it has been common to regard the irreversible cessation of *brain* functions as both necessary and sufficient for death to occur. One attraction of this view is that it is certain that brain-dead people will never regain consciousness or manifest any of the characteristic marks of personhood. However, earlier confidence that brain-death would be relatively easy to determine by a variety of tests has recently been sapped by disputes over the appropriate diagnostic criteria to be applied, as well as controversy over whether brain-death should be defined in terms of the cessation of whole brain, brain stem or higher brain functions.[4] An additional complication is that other physical functions of brain-dead people can sometimes be kept going by artificial means. Referring to the work of the physiologist Alan Shewmon, the philosopher Jeff McMahan cites the case of a brain-dead boy in Florida who, at his parents' behest, has been artificially ventilated, fed and hydrated for over fourteen years, during which time his body has grown and recovered from infections and wounds. In this period, too, his brain has become replaced by "ghost-like tissues and disorganized proteinaceous fluids" (McMahan 2002: 430). We might be inclined to press criterion (2) from the President's Commission report and say that this youth is really dead. Michael Leming and George Dickinson remark of such cases that "If the brain is dead, any artificially induced heartbeat is merely pumping blood through a dead body" (2002: 43). On the other hand, it may seem counter-intuitive to describe as "dead" a body that exhibits many of the normal functions of indubitably living bodies, even if they are not being normally sustained. This reflection may lead us, as it leads McMahan (2002: 429–30), to conclude that brain-death is not, after all, sufficient for the death of the human organism. Yet this conclusion is perhaps resistible. The concept of a living organism, although not precise, nevertheless implies a system possessing at least a modicum of functional integrity and self-sufficiency or spontaneity. In this sense, the tragic youth in Florida may be denied to be a living organism. Perhaps the simplest way of resolving the tension is to allow that the concept of death is not univocal, and that a distinction can be made between the death of an organism and the death of a body (although it is obvious that in the vast majority of cases, these concepts will coincide in their application).

We also need to decide what to say about people whose brains are partly dead, or irretrievably damaged, and who remain in a persistent vegetative state (PVS), some at least of their vital bodily functions being sustained only by life-support equipment. By more stringent forms of the brain-death criterion, such patients are plainly still alive, having some brain functions remaining, although they have ceased to be conscious subjects of a life.

One response to such cases would be to abandon the normally unquestioned assumption that death is an all-or-nothing affair. Perhaps we should describe PVS subjects as occupying a halfway house between life and death, analogous to the way in which we might describe twilight as a state between day and night. (This would not, of course, be at all the same as being "half dead" in the metaphorical and jocular sense in which we often describe a weary or worn-out person by that phrase.) As failure of brain function is a matter of degree, it may seem reasonable to regard life and death as being matters of degree too, so that someone who has reached a certain point of decline might be deemed to be more dead than alive. Rationally considered, it seems distinctly odd to describe a PVS patient whose brain retains only 1 per cent of its normal functional capacity as fully alive just because his brain is not yet quite dead. We do not say that it is day right up to the point when the very last perceptible light has gone. Although, admittedly, there would be certain legal and forensic difficulties in the way of classifying some subjects as neither wholly alive nor wholly dead (for instance, we would need to decide what kind of legal protection and rights should be accorded in these intermediate cases), there seems to be no compelling reason for rejecting a conceptual shift that would permit more nuanced descriptions to be given of a subject's state. A further consequence of accepting this change is that we should see dying, in some instances, not as a process that terminates in the sudden event of death but as a process in which life is gradually extinguished. That we conventionally look on death as an absolute condition rather than one that comes in degrees is most probably a vestige of the old belief that death occurs all at once, at the moment when the soul leaves the body. On this view, while dying can be an extended process, the event of death is instantaneous. But if that traditional belief is abandoned, as I shall argue in the next section it should be, there is much less reason to reject the idea of "twilight" states of life and death.[5]

Would the notion of an intermediate life–death state also help us to characterize the case of Wilbur, whose body has been cryogenically preserved immediately after its vital functions have ceased, in the hope that future medical developments will enable it to be restored to life and health? No, because in Wilbur all vital processes have come entirely to a stop. We might alternatively consider describing Wilbur as being in a state of suspended animation. However, this description only sidesteps the issue of whether Wilbur, in his deep-frozen condition, is alive or dead. Wilbur is not currently animated any more than a parked car that is in a state of suspended motion is currently moving. Given Wilbur's present non-animation (the absence of all vital functions), the question recurs of whether his state should be classified as one of death. Suppose that medical technology never advances sufficiently for it to be possible to thaw him out and repair the organs that have failed, and that he remains in his deep-frozen state for centuries. Should we say that Wilbur's death has been indefinitely postponed? Or should we regard him as having died when his vital organs originally shut down? Again, imagine that a careless technician accidentally switches off the refrigeration equipment five years after Wilbur has been frozen, and that his thawing body starts to decay. Is this the point of Wilbur's death, or has he already been dead for half a decade?

It is not clear that these questions have a right answer. Our notions of death and dying have evolved in contexts in which the possibility of cryogenic preservation techniques was never envisaged. Consequently, their employment in the new context is problematic and can only be sorted out by means of stipulative decisions. The main objection to saying that someone in Wilbur's position has died *before* his body is deep frozen is that any future restoration to health would then amount to a resurrection of Wilbur from the dead. But would that description really be so very objectionable? It would, if it were essential to our concept of death that death was irreversible. But this seems rather doubtful. Most people who hear the gospel account of Jesus's raising of the dead Lazarus, whether or not they find it credible, do not find it incoherent. It appears to be an empirical question, and not one to be settled *a priori*, whether there can be any return from that "undiscover'd country, from whose bourn no traveller [normally] returns" (*Hamlet* III.i). Conceivably, one day cryogenic techniques will make the return from the dead not only possible but even common, at least among rich decedents.

The alternative is to say that a person in Wilbur's condition does not die unless or until he starts to decay. But this choice comes at a high price. It means that someone, say, whose organs fail while he is lost in the Arctic wilderness and whose body freezes before putrefaction can set in must also be allowed to be still alive! (It is possible, after all, that in two hundred years' time his body will be recovered and its animation restored.) For it is not a defensible view that the *intention* behind cryogenic freezing makes the difference to whether Wilbur is dead or alive. Indeed, on this line of thought, the mere act of freezing or otherwise preserving intact a body whose vital processes have ceased is sufficient to keep death at bay and provide a sort of immortality. I suspect that few people would take much comfort from this method of "cheating death" or feel much attraction for this development of the concept.

It was suggested above that the concept of death is not univocal and that we might wish to distinguish between the ideas of the death of the organism and the death of the body. These concepts have in common that they represent a biological perspective on death. But it is obvious that we do not think about the contrast between life and death in exclusively biological terms. Indeed, our dominant outlook on death – and the main reason why we regard the prospect of our own demise as so distasteful – is that we see death as the end of us as selves, or persons. McMahan (2002: 425) puts this in provocative, but defensible, terms by saying that we can die before our organisms do. (So now it appears that selves can die before organisms, and organisms before bodies.) It sometimes happens, when someone, as a result of illness or accident, is no longer capable of higher brain functions and is in a state of irreversible coma, kept clinically alive on a life-support machine, that his family and friends think and speak of him as dead. This should be seen neither, on the one hand, as confusion nor, on the other, as mere metaphor. Whether we prefer to think of a person as McMahan does (*ibid.*: 423–6 and *passim*), as an embodied mind, or, as Peter Strawson recommended (1959: ch.3), as an inseparable complex of physical and mental properties, we will see the person as at an end once the higher mental operations have ceased and permanent unconsciousness commenced.

Certainly, PVS patients who are kept alive by life-support equipment are sometimes regarded by their friends and relatives as being in a state akin to that of deep sleep; moreover, on rare occasions patients who have remained in a state of profound coma for years have recovered some level of consciousness, an event that resembles waking up. Yet where serious and irreversible injury has occurred to the brain and central nervous system it is simply wrong to see the patient's condition as a kind of sleep. People who are asleep do not cease to be persons, but those who have ceased to be persons, having lost all capacity for the higher mental functions, are not asleep (nor, we might add, do the dead, as they are sometimes said to, sleep in their graves).

Is there survival of death?

People sometimes confuse the notion of survival of death with that of personal immortality. In fact there are two reasons why these should be distinguished. One is that if it is intelligible to suppose that something of us might survive, whatever survives might conceivably be less than is necessary to count as *us*: for instance, it might be no more than a ghostly shade without intelligence or self-consciousness. The other is that even if we were to retain full personal status after the death of our body, it is a further supposition that we would survive for eternity, or for any considerable length of time. In a poignant scene in James Elroy Flecker's play *Hassan*, the ghosts of the lovers Rafi and Pervaneh, who had chosen death in preference to separation, outlast their execution only briefly before fading away. We cannot simply assume that ghosts or spirits, if there should be any, have staying power.

Although recently in decline, a belief in some form of survival of death has been a remarkably prevalent feature of human societies since historical records began. Even before that, Neanderthal communities appear from the archaeological evidence to have practised funeral rites, possibly indicative of a belief that the dead were not wholly gone. Often, of course, the view that there is life after death has been grounded in religious traditions, although we should not suppose that all religions, even in the West, have preached a message of personal survival (early Judaism, for instance, did not). Religious reasons for believing in an afterlife are characteristically of a very different kind to the arguments typically offered by philosophers. In David Hume's view (1963: esp. 263, 270), no philosophical considerations were adequate to establish the reality of an afterlife, the credibility of which, if any, must therefore rely solely on religious revelation.[6] But even religious claims can be subjected to philosophical critique in respect of their coherence and consistency. Any claim that there is life after death, however august its origin, needs to be accompanied by some account of the mechanics of survival. It has to be explained precisely *what* survives (a soul? a spirit? an astral body?), and how this can resist the forces of dissolution that destroy the bodily frame. We also need to be assured that whatever survives is not a mere trace of the ante-mortem subject but in essence *is* that person, and neither a sub-person nor a different person. In addition, those religions that hold that only human beings survive death, and not animals, need to explain what constitutes the crucial difference between them. Any such account inevitably ventures on to the territory of philosophy (and maybe that of more empirical disciplines as well), and is legitimately subjected to extra-religious standards of credibility.

On the face of it, the belief in survival is implausible. If ever a claim were in need of careful philosophical pleading, this would seem to be it. When a person dies, his or her body loses all signs of animation and ordinarily soon starts to decay. Those who hold that nevertheless the person survives in some invisible and intangible form do so in spite of the obvious appearances. The burden of proof is therefore on them to make good their claim, rather than on those who deny it to disprove it; and we shall see that this is a hard burden to bear.

The most popular philosophical way to defend the belief in survival has been via a view of a person as a composite of a material body and an immaterial mind or soul, a position known as "dualism". Dualism comes in various forms, some of which are more favourable than others to the idea of disembodied survival. In order to support a belief in survival, a dualistic theory needs to satisfy three conditions. First, it must represent the mind or soul as capable of an existence independent of and separate from the body. Secondly, it must conceive the mental part of a person as being immaterial in nature, and therefore immune to any processes of physical decay. And thirdly, it needs to identify the essence of the person with the mental, rather than the corporeal, component, otherwise it will be unable to justify the claim that bodily death is not the end of the person.

Not every form of dualism fulfils all three conditions. Thus some dualists have supposed that a person is an inextricable compound of mental and physical elements, so intimately bound together that the dissolution of one component inevitably involves the termination of the other. On this view, even though mind and its states are immaterial, they are unable to exist apart from the body and cannot survive its death. Another kind of dualism maintains that the mind is to be identified not with some substance or substratum that *has* thoughts, sensations and other mental states, but with the "bundle" of mental contents themselves. Typically, bundle theories explain self-identity in one or other of two ways: either in terms of the unifying content of the items in the bundle, where they represent a single and continuous point of view; or by reference to their association with a particular physical body. Clearly, the latter criterion would not be available in the case of posthumous bundles. It is perhaps just imaginable that a bundle of unified mental states might exist beyond a person's death but it is hard to explain what would hold them together and preserve the synoptic viewpoint in the absence of any relation of items in the bundle to either a mental substratum (*ex hypothesi*) or a physical organism.

The version of dualism best fitted to support the thesis of personal survival is the one defended by Plato and at a later date (if not always quite consistently) by Descartes. In his dialogue the *Phaedo*, Plato presented a dualistic theory that satisfies each of the three conditions outlined above. According to this account, a person is not a compound of body and soul but a soul inhabiting a body, from which it will float free at death. Defining death as "the separation of the soul from the body", Plato describes death as occurring when "the body separates from the soul, and remains by itself apart from the soul, and the soul, separated from the body, exists by itself apart from the body" (*Phaedo* 64c; 1956b: 467). Because dying marks not the end of the self but its liberation, as Plato expresses it, from the chains of the body, it is a moment to be looked forward to rather than dreaded by the person of philosophical temperament. For as soon as we are "pure and rid of the body's foolishness", we can start indulging in the pursuit of knowledge without distraction. To those who love wisdom, therefore, "death ... is the least terrible thing in the world" (*Phaedo* 67a, 67e; 1956b: 470).[7]

Plato's cheery vision of a delightful afterlife of philosophical speculation (delightful, at least, for those so inclined) depends on a number of highly doubtful assumptions. Despite the confidence with which he insists on the ability of the soul to exist independently of the body, the hypothesis of an immaterial substance without physical attributes both is obscure in itself and raises the notorious problem of how such a substance can interact causally with the material body. Although Descartes speculated that the pineal gland at the base of the brain was the point of contact between mind and brain, the main difficulty is to understand how an event in immaterial substance (say, my forming an intention to type the word "dualism") can give rise to a series of events in the physical world (certain happenings in my brain and muscles, followed by the appearance of the word "dualism" on my computer screen). Such a theory also offends against the thesis of the causal closure of the material world, that is, the claim that events in the physical world have sufficient physical causes and admit of no others. (Note that any qualification this claim may require in the light of the discovery of causal indeterminacy at the quantum level supplies no comfort at all to believers in immaterial causality.)

In any case, as everyday experience tells us and scientific investigation confirms, the mental life of both human beings and animals appears causally dependent on the functioning of the physical organism. People whose sense organs are defective have limited perceptual capacities, while serious injuries to the brain may produce dementia. One wonders what Plato would make of those unfortunate people who, as the result of brain and neural damage, are reduced to existing in a persistent vegetative state. If Plato's story is true, it is puzzling why such physical damage should be accompanied by the seeming shutdown of the conscious and intelligent soul; if the soul were truly independent and self-sufficient it ought to be able to carry on its functions regardless of what was going on in the body. Since Plato speaks of the body "enchaining" the soul, he would probably suggest that the liberated soul resumes its activity on the death of such unfortunates. However, it is stretching credulity very far to suppose that the soul cannot function properly when part of the brain is damaged but is at its liveliest in the absence of all brain activity whatever.

It must be admitted that much more needs to be said about mind and its relationship to matter before the issue of personal survival of death can be finally closed. But it is fair to remark that theories of mind that are currently popular with philosophers, such as functionalism or the "anomalous monism" defended by Donald Davidson, offer no basis for supposing that persons can survive their physical deaths. While such theories are more sophisticated than earlier versions of materialism (Davidson's, for instance, concedes that discourse about our mental life is not translatable into discourse about brain and neural states, and is governed by a different set of principles), they firmly reject the idea of non-material substance.[8] Viewing persons as essentially, and not merely contingently, embodied, they leave no room for their survival as souls or spirits. Most contemporary philosophy of mind is thus deeply inhospitable to notions of an afterlife, and poses challenges to the coherence and credibility of the notion that have not been, and on present showing seem unlikely to be, met.

Before we leave the topic of the (im)probability of an afterlife, we should look briefly at a quite different idea of survival (although arguably the word "survival" should be placed within scare quotes). Although they have not been widely popular in the West, theories of reincarnation and of the transmigration of souls (technically known as "metempsychosis") have enjoyed considerable support in some cultures. The idea that, as Shakespeare put it, "the soul of our grandam might haply inhabit a bird" (*Twelfth Night*, IV.ii) was also upheld by the ancient Pythagoreans and may have had some influence on Plato. Theories of this type are fundamentally dualist, with the special twist that souls are held to have existed for ever and to possess the ability to migrate from body to body. Commonly an ethical strand is entwined with the metaphysical account, whereby the moral quality of a soul's existence in one bodily container is held to determine whether its next incarnation will be as a lower or higher creature. (This explains why our grandmother, if she has behaved badly during her human life, might be born next time as a bird.) The most desirable fate for a soul is finally to abandon its earthly existence and separate identity and to be absorbed into the Absolute, conceived of as a kind of world or universal soul.

Theories of reincarnation raise many and obvious philosophical difficulties. They are, to start with, uncompromisingly dualist theories, and pose the problems we have already encountered in connection with more familiar views that maintain the independent existence of immaterial substance. Another difficulty is the sheer unverifiability of the claims that souls drift between different bodily vessels, and that one and the same soul can animate, at different times, creatures as disparate as a human being, a mosquito and a dog. (Some philosophical critics would go further and deny that such identity claims were even meaningful.) What could souls be *like*, in respect of their basic characteristics, to be so infinitely adaptable? If the thrush that sings on the tree in my garden was once my grandmother, then what core or essential properties has it carried through this profound transformation? Unless souls can be assigned some individuating qualities it is impossible to say what would make them the *same* souls throughout the course of their migrations. (Evidently they do not retain the same power of thought or the same perceptual capacities as they pass from bearer to bearer.) Alternatively, if we suppose that they have no individuating properties and are mere spiritual substrata that acquire different sets of qualities in different phases of their existence, then it no longer makes sense – contrary to the hypothesis – to talk of a plurality of distinct souls; instead, there is effectively only undifferentiated soul-substance. Aristotle once remarked that only someone in the grip of a theory would believe such-and-such a proposition. We may say that only someone in the grip of a religious doctrine would believe in reincarnation, since philosophical reasoning from a secular standpoint is quite unable to make it plausible.

We began this section by noting the distinction between the ideas of survival of death and of personal immortality. The notion of immortality faces all the difficulties that confront the idea of survival of death, plus some extra ones. Whatever of us survives our deaths, if anything does, must be of a very special and unusual kind to be capable of lasting for ever. Since nothing else of any structural complexity within our experience possesses such a remarkable power, we may reasonably ask what grounds there are for supposing that our posthumous selves are so very different.

The favourite move that philosophers wishing to defend the idea of eternal life have made is to argue that the soul, being composed of spiritual substance, is not subject to damage or decay in the manner of material things. This is the argument offered, for instance, by Plato in the *Phaedo*. According to him, only composite things that have parts are subject to dissolution and decay. The soul, however, unlike the body, is a simple entity, without parts, and therefore imperishable. And being imperishable, it must last for ever.[9] In other words, souls are never-ending because there is nothing that can ever go wrong with them.

But how, we may ask, can Plato be so sure of this? How does he know that spiritual substance does not wear out in time, even if it takes a very long time? All the analogies of our experience suggest that nothing is of infinite duration. Moreover, in the absence of a detailed account of what the soul is like, the proposal that it has no parts appears a mere ungrounded assumption. Obviously, on a dualist view, the soul has no *physical* parts, but Plato's imperishability thesis requires the further, implausible premise that the soul, notwithstanding its ability to carry out complex mental operations, has no internal structure at all. But even if we were willing to grant the less than perspicuous claim that the soul is a simple substance, it would still be unclear why such a substance should not eventually decline or fade away.

Most people who believe in the immortality of the soul are likely to rest their belief on a religious rather than a philosophical basis. Perhaps God has constructed us with (or *as*) souls of an indestructible type, in order that we shall dwell with him in heaven for eternity (or at least those of us who come up to the mark morally). Yet some philosophers have questioned whether survival for eternity would really be a good thing for us. Several writers, following the lead of Bernard Williams (1973b), have argued that eternal life would be eternally tedious, and that we would not be able to preserve a sense of a meaningful existence when anything that we might think of doing could always be put off to another day, or another millennium. How persuasive such arguments are we shall investigate in Chapter 3.

Leaving religious considerations aside, it is hard to dispute that philosophical attempts to defend the belief in either the survival of death or in personal immortality have been somewhat less than convincing. That being the case, I shall proceed in this book on the assumption that death is the end of us as distinct and self-conscious selves. To readers who are indisposed to accept this view, or who wish to leave the door open to the possibility that an afterlife of some sort exists, I would stress that it is a working assumption I am making rather than a dogmatic assertion, although one that is justified, I think, on the balance of the arguments. Perhaps, after all, I am wrong, and we do survive our deaths. But since it would be hard to write a book on death without taking a stand on issues of survival and immortality, I shall presume in what follows that death is personal extinction, and that the various ethical and existential questions that the prospect of death raises are most profitably viewed from this perspective.

First- and third-person perspectives: the social context of death

In his famous story "The Death of Ivan Ilych", Leo Tolstoy describes how Ivan, a prosperous and well-respected judge, who is dying from a terminal illness, realizes with a shock the fact of his own mortality:

> The syllogism he had learnt from Kiezewetter's Logic: "Caius is a man, men are mortal, therefore Caius is mortal" had always seemed to him correct as applied to Caius, but certainly not as applied to himself. That Caius – man in the abstract – was mortal, was perfectly correct, but he was not Caius, not an abstract man, but a creature quite, quite separate from all the others. (Tolstoy 1960: 131–2)

As Ivan recalls his past life, the acts, thoughts, feelings and relationships that have made him distinct from anyone else, the idea of his own death seems almost impossible to comprehend: "for me, little Vanya, Ivan Ilych, with all my thoughts and emotions, it's altogether a different matter. It cannot be that I ought to die. That would be too terrible" (*ibid.*: 132).

Ivan's predicament illustrates an important fact about death and dying that has received a considerable amount of philosophical attention: it is one thing to think about death in the abstract, or in a third-person way about the deaths of others, and a quite different thing to contemplate the prospect of one's own demise. Reflecting on my own death is hard, as Ivan found, because I cannot readily imagine the world without *me*. I can imagine, for example, observing my own funeral, but when I do so I am not really imagining myself as dead, but rather as a living onlooker. Before we can feel existentially troubled about the fact we will die, we first need to grasp it.

Once we do so, death may seem to be an exceedingly lonely affair. Heidegger remarks that no one else can do our dying for us. The loneliness is not just psychological but logical: necessarily, only *I* can die *my* death. Caius dies Caius's death, and Ivan dies Ivan's. Nevertheless it is sometimes said, and with some justice, that philosophers have focused overmuch on the analysis of death's significance from the first-person standpoint and have paid too little attention to the social meanings of death and dying. Before we go on, in Chapter 2, to discuss some of the existential questions that arise when we confront, or try to, the reality of our own being-towards-death (to use Heidegger's phrase), it is worth saying a little more about the social and cultural dimensions of death.

Because we are social animals, we are characteristically involved in a host of different, criss-crossing and overlapping relationships with other people, some intimate and private, others more impersonal and public. When we die, our death disrupts this extensive set of relationships, forcing a greater or lesser reconstruction of the social web. While my death may matter most of all to me, it will certainly not matter only to me unless I have lived a quite unusually solitary life. This is not an expression of egotism but a candid recognition of the social situation. Robert Solomon has criticized as "morbid solipsism" the outlook of writers who fashion an image of death "solely in terms of the self" (1998: 175). Death marks the end of my existence, but I care about that, suggests Solomon, because in dying I break my relationships with others. What authors such as Heidegger tend to ignore is that: "I want to live because of other people. I want to live because I love, because I am steeped in my projects – social projects, as Sartre above all would be the first to appreciate. ... I am part of [others'] world as they are part of mine" (*ibid*.: 176).

Solomon's claim that we care that we shall die, and about how we shall die, primarily because we care about others should not be understood as suggesting that our predominant concern is with other people *rather* than ourselves; the truth is that we care about ourselves in relation to others and about others in relation to ourselves. It would be quite wrong to think of one's own death as if it had nothing to do with anyone else. A person's death is a significant shared or social event, as well as a momentous private one. A person who dies will be a parent, child, lover, breadwinner, dependant, role model or hate figure, paragon or pariah, engine-driver, doctor, priest, man about town or woman in the country, a player in a wide variety of meshing dramas. Ivan Ilych was a husband, a father and a keen bridge-player as well as a member of the judicial bench. When an individual dies, a part of society dies too, with sometimes far-reaching consequences for the rest of the social organism. Addressing the dislocation caused by death requires multiple recasting of parts and rewriting of scripts.

While death in any society compels a process of readjustment, in which the relationships fractured by an individual's death are remodelled or replaced, the details of the process vary widely from one social environment to another. Sociologists and anthropologists who study death in different cultures emphasize the very disparate nature of the ways in which people understand death and come to terms with it.

Much of what is felt and done naturally depends on what the members of particular cultures believe about the situation of the dead *vis-à-vis* the living. In the view of many traditional societies, the deceased remain in existence as ghosts or spirits with a continuing interest in the affairs of the community. (They are, so to speak, the emeritus members of society.) The dead are often perceived as able to affect the fortunes of the living, and as such needing to be honoured and propitiated to secure their goodwill. For instance, native Hawaiians believe that they stand in a symbiotic relationship to their departed ancestors, who act as guardians to their living descendants provided they have been granted a proper burial (Ayau 2002). In some Native American cultures, for example, the Pawnee, it is thought that disturbing the buried remains of the dead causes their spirits to become restless and harmful (Riding In 2000).

It has been much less common in Western societies, even among people who believe in an afterlife, to think that the dead can or do intervene in the affairs of the living. Nevertheless, elaborate funeral ceremonies and mourning rites have often been practised, without any view to placating the dead. To the question why people go to so much trouble when they do not expect the dead to respond, Rai Gaita suggests a simple answer: "The belief that we should be true to the dead goes deep in the human heart" (2004: 87). Even if the dead are quite unaware of what we do for them, our rituals and mourning are a way of showing them respect. While they may also help the living survivors of the broken relationships to attain a sense of psychological closure, Gaita thinks that this is a secondary function, and one made possible only by the participants' sense that they are doing what they do primarily for the deceased (*ibid.*: 86). Gaita's observation is an acute one, even if it casts some doubts on the rationality of the funerary practices of disbelievers in an after-life, who on this reading of their motives are acting for the sake of people who they think no longer exist. But we may postpone to a later chapter the broader question of whether it makes any sense to ascribe interests to the dead, or to consider that they can be post-humously helped or harmed.

It may seem that there is nothing more spontaneous than the emotions that arise when someone we love dies: generally grief and a sense of loss or emptiness; often a feeling that life has lost part of its meaning for us; perhaps also a fear or dislike of facing the future by ourselves. Bereaved people sometimes report hav-ing, too, an unreasonable (and guilt-inducing) resentment that the loved one has deserted them by dying. Yet the way in which death is experienced in different societies varies more than we might have expected before consulting the anthropological evidence. Death may be universal in that it comes to all, but it is not – phenomeno-logically, psychologically, socially – a uniform occurrence across the human species. Nor do the differences have to do merely with the overt and ritualistic expressions of mourning, or the modes of disposing of the physical remains. Thus Norbert Elias writes that:

> Not only means of communication or patterns of constraint, but the experience of death, too, can differ from society to society. It is variable and group-specific; no matter how natural and immutable it seems to members of each particular society, it has been learned. (1985: 4–5)

In different environments death may be seen as triumph or tragedy, ultimate fulfilment or frustration, irretrievable loss or a happy release, the end of life or the gateway to a new one, a semicolon in existence or the final full-stop, a moment for lamenting or for celebration, an *adieu* or an *au revoir*.

Even within the same society, death may be experienced differently and accorded divergent meanings. The archaeologist Sarah Tarlow, who has devoted much time to the comparative study of past communities' responses to mortality, reminds us that "within our own society there is a huge range of metaphors, emotions, rituals and practices through which people understand bereavement and mortality" (1999: xii). This is in part because we no longer have a single eschatology in common: there are a number of competing models for understanding the fate of the dead. It also reflects the fact that our modern Western world is a very complex one, standing as it does at the confluence of several cultural streams that have not perfectly merged (and are not likely to in the foreseeable future, as society becomes increasingly multicultural).

Although a disposition to feel such emotions as grief, anger, fear or jealousy is plausibly seen as a species universal, our natural emotional responses are susceptible to being trained, focused, moulded and manipulated by external forces. It is overly reductive to view emotions, as some cultural anthropologists have done, as social constructs, the objects and modes of expression of which are entirely dependent on conditioning by our community. Yet it would also be wrong to discount or downplay the cultural malleability of natural human emotion, the plasticity that allows attitudes to the ancestors to range from love and respect in some societies to hatred and fear in others. How one feels about the dead is inevitably affected by what one believes about them; and it makes a big difference whether one looks on the deceased as benevolent, affectionate guardians, or as envious and malicious ghosts, or as non-existent.

That death is a social as well as an individual phenomenon is a truth that we must bear in mind throughout this study. Provided we do so, we should be less in danger of succumbing to the "morbid solipsism" that Solomon claims to find in the work of many philosophers. But there is no denying the importance of the first-person perspective on death or its centrality in any philosophical treatment of the subject. Our knowledge that we shall die and the realization of our own finitude are distinctively human features that mark us off from other species. They shape our attitudes to our lives and profoundly affect the kinds of persons that we become. Some people feel considerable existential distress, amounting sometimes to dread, at the thought of their forthcoming death; others view the prospect of their end more calmly or stoically, although probably no one ever does so completely dispassionately. Of course, most of us are not constantly dwelling on the thought that we shall die; there are far too many other things in life that require our attention for *that*. Yet if the idea of our mortality is not generally at the forefront of our minds, it is there in the background as one of the constituents of our specifically human form of self-awareness. If we compare a life to a piece of music, it is a recurrent leitmotif – or, better, a ground-bass – running through the composition. It would only be a slight exaggeration to say that life is built around it.

This being the case, it is worth looking in more depth at the first-person perspective on death, and at some of the ethical and existential questions that confront us when we reflect on what it means for *us* to die. These important topics will therefore form the subject of Chapter 2.

2 | Existential perspectives

The anticipation of death

> And he spake a parable unto them, saying, The ground of a certain man brought forth plentifully: And he thought within himself, saying, What shall I do, because I have no room where to bestow my fruits? And he said, This will I do: I will pull down my barns, and build greater; and there will I bestow all my fruits and my goods. And I will say to my soul, Soul, thou hast much goods laid up for many years; take thine ease, eat, drink, and be merry. But God said unto him, Thou fool, this night thy soul shall be required of thee: then whose shall those things be, which thou hast provided? (Luke 12:16–20)

This well-known parable prefigures a theme common in the literature of existentialism. According to a recent commentator on Heidegger: "we typically flee in the face of death. We regard death as something that happens primarily to others, whom we think of as simply more cases or instances of death, as if they were mere tokens of an essentially impersonal type" (Mulhall 2005: 130). And that appears to be just what the parable's rich man does: he pretends that death does not concern him, ignoring the fact that it could arrive at any time without announcement.

Existentialist writers lay particular stress on the need for individuals to recognize unflinchingly the conditions under which they live in the world. Since, on the existentialist view, each of us bears the sole responsibility for determining what sort of person to be and what acts to perform, it is crucially important that in making our choices we are careful to avoid all forms of comforting self-delusion. The rich man's outlook is, in this sense, "inauthentic" because he fails to acknowledge the inescapable temporal bounded-ness of his life: the fact that his form of being is, in Heidegger's phrase, "being-towards-death". In contrast, the authentic person recognizes that the continuance of life is utterly contingent and death an ever-present possibility (Heidegger 1962: Division 2, part 1). While authenticity does not require that one should dwell obses-sively on thoughts of death, the certainty *that* death will occur com-bined with uncertainty over *when* it will occur inevitably makes it an object of anxious anticipation (*ibid.*: 302).

Admittedly, there is an element of anachronism in our reading the gospel story this way. Its original intended moral was that the wealthy farmer, in focusing on his worldly fortunes, had foolishly neglected to store up treasure for himself in heaven. Still, the par-able serves to illustrate Heidegger's claim that people typically try to tranquillize themselves in the face of death, speciously reasoning that because it is "proximally not yet present-at-hand" for them, it is "therefore no threat" (*ibid.*: 297). Indeed, Heidegger's criti-cism of common attitudes to death goes further than this. Popular wisdom maintains that it is cowardly to concern ourselves much about death and that only the faint-hearted dwell on the thought of their own end. To Heidegger, this is a serious moral inversion because it diverts us from a proper recognition of our existential predicament. "*The 'they'* [i.e. 'the public']", he complains, "*does not permit us the courage for anxiety in the face of death*" (*ibid.*: 298, original emphasis). What is represented as bravery is actually an unheroic evasion of a truth that is of the deepest personal import for each and every one of us.

Heidegger's claim that we are guilty, in our state of chronic inauthenticity, of a moral inversion should not, though, be accepted without question. Can St Luke's farmer, who looks forward to many more years of prosperous life, really be charged with anything worse than an overabundance of optimism? Leaving to one side the religious dimension of the story, it could reasonably be argued that in planning the enlargement of his barns he is simply doing what any person of practical good sense would do: providing for his future on the working assumption (in the absence of evidence to the contrary) that he will have one. Jesus himself in other places commends those who show a certain measure of worldly wisdom (in, for example, the parable of the unjust steward, who, on the eve of being dismissed from service, curries favour with his master's debtors; Luke 16:1–13). In the words of the eighteenth-century theologian Jonathan Edwards, "we are not obliged to behave ourselves as though we concluded that we should not live to another day". If everyone acted on *that* assumption, then no one would make provision for his temporal subsistence and "at this rate, the whole world would presently murder itself" (Edwards 1788: 299).[1] In Aesop's fable of the ant and the grasshopper, it is the ant, which works through the year to put by food for the hard times, that is praised for prudence, not the grasshopper, which dances the summer away and starves in the winter.

It would be wrong, however, to suppose that there were only two choices before us: either to dwell on thoughts of our impending death to the extent that our life becomes poisoned and paralysed, or to refuse altogether to think of it in connection with ourselves. It is quite possible to maintain a lively consciousness of our mortality without our having to treat each new moment as though it might be our last. (Edwards remarks that "[n]ot depending on another day, is a different thing from concluding, that we shall not live another day" [*ibid.*: 298].) And there is no good reason to judge it a cowardly evasion of the reality of our situation to draw up plans for the future. On the contrary, as other strands in existentialist thinking have emphasized, we define ourselves by our activity in the world and would be guilty of bad faith if we framed no projects for the future on the grounds that we were passively waiting for the death that might arrive at any moment.

I remember once reading about an old man, well past his hundredth year, who woke up each morning with the thought "Still here?" When one reaches extreme old age, it is obviously foolish to bank on having many more days of life. At any age we need to form a realistic estimate of the probabilities of seeing another dawn. When the probability of doing so is high, it is silly to suppose it to be otherwise. However – as Heidegger rightly stresses – it is also self-deceitful to pretend it to be a certainty. But how much anxiety should we feel about this, and on precisely what grounds? Should a centenarian, whose chance of seeing another year is considerably less than that of a fifty-year-old, feel more anxiety because of the greater proximity of death, or less on account of (in Heideggerian language) the diminishing *"indefiniteness* of its 'when'"? It might be suggested that the very old have less reason than the young or middle-aged to be anxious about death, since they have been fortunate enough to have had the time they needed to fulfil themselves. On the other hand, there is something especially tragic about a long life that has *not* been a fulfilled one, and that is now too close to its end to redeem. Although we often colloquially remark of some elderly person that he or she has "had a good innings",[2] we must be careful not to confuse quantity of time with quality. Long lives are not always better than short ones.

Nevertheless, the person who dies, whether young or old, loses everything. In the *Tractatus Logico-Philosophicus*, Wittgenstin shrewdly observes that "at death the world does not alter, but comes to an end" (1969: §6.431). Of course, we recognize that the objective world will go on without us; other people will continue to live in a world that does not finish when we do. We show that we care about this when we make arrangements for the well-being of our descendants or decide on the posthumous disposal of our goods. But Wittgenstein is not speaking merely in metaphor. Rather, he is making the point that the world *for me* is over with my death. The world as I know it is the world that is presented through my own consciousness. As Herbert Fingarette says, from the first-person point of view, "death plainly takes on momentous import". My death is not simply the exit of an actor from the stage. "When I cease to be, that whole world that I live – its space, its time and all they contain – disappears" (1996: 30).[3] In this subjective perspective, I and the world are one and they exist and disappear together.

The loss of my world along with myself may appear to be a substantial ground of existential anxiety, yet we should be wary of arriving at this conclusion too briskly. After all, if *I* cease to be simultaneously with my conscious world, then there is no subject any more to whom any tragic loss can be ascribed. And to say that *I* will suffer from the loss of myself is, on the face of it, incoherent. The Epicurean insight that death marks the end of the subject poses a difficulty for the claim that death should be anticipated with intense anxiety. It is not just that, as Wittgenstein says, "Death is not an event in life: we do not live to experience death". To speak of *loss* in this context is additionally paradoxical because a loss requires a loser. Yet clearly there is no loss of life before death, while afterwards there is no longer a subject to face and experience loss. This is the point of Wittgenstein's immediately following remark that "Our life has no end in just the way in which our visual field has no limits" (1969: §6.4311). In the same way as we cannot see beyond our visual field (since this is the frame within which all our seeing is done), we shall never be in the position of subjects whose lives have ended.

In spite of these reflections on the import of the loss of the subject at death, the claim that our forthcoming death is the legitimate focus of existential anxiety can be defended. For although, once dead, I shall not be around to have a tragic sense of what I have lost, prior to my death I can regret the fact that the world of my consciousness will come to an end, and that there will be nothing to matter to me any more. Unless my existence is for contingent reasons an utterly miserable one with no hope of improvement, its end is not something I can welcome. Indeed, even if my life is one of unrelieved suffering, I may still wish it to continue in preference to the ending of my universe. Even a literally hellish existence may seem better than none at all. In John Milton's *Paradise Lost*, the fallen angel Belial poses the question:

> ... for who would lose,
> Though full of pain, this intellectual being,
> Those thoughts that wander through eternity,
> To perish rather, swallowed up and lost
> In the wide womb of uncreated night,
> Devoid of sense and motion?
>
> (*Paradise Lost*, book II, lines 146–51)

No doubt, despite Belial's rhetoric, there are those who would prefer extinction to misery, and some people resort to suicide as an exit from an existence that has become intolerable. But Belial's question reminds us that the value of our lives to us is not a simple function of the amount of pleasure and pain they contain. It must also be considered that when our lives end we disappear into what Milton calls "the wide womb of uncreated night" and Peter Loptson, in a more modern idiom calls "the black hole of non-being" (1998: 140); and this is a high price to pay for losing our pain.

We shall return in Chapter 5 to discuss more fully the Epicurean contention that death can be neither an evil nor a good in the absence of a subject. If Epicurus is right, and the "evil" of death is an illusion born of a misunderstanding of the nature of death, then the claim that the prospect of death is properly looked on with existential anxiety will need to be revisited. Meanwhile we may note the ironic fact that the very feature of death – the extinction of the subject – that in Epicurus's view makes death non-fearful, is precisely the feature that justifies, in some other writers' eyes, our awaiting our deaths with particular existential anxiety.

Death as our "ownmost possibility"

We have made reference to Heidegger several times in the previous section and must now take a closer look at the views of a philosopher whose discussion of death from an existential viewpoint has proved one of the most seminal – if also one of the most controversial – of the past hundred years. Alasdair MacIntyre has complained that too many philosophers in the Western tradition have ignored facts about "our vulnerabilities and afflictions and [facts] concerning the extent of our dependence on particular others", as though moral agents were "continuously rational, healthy and untroubled" beings (MacIntyre 1999: 1–2). Not so Heidegger, who acknowledges the plentiful grounds of anxiety that beset us in our human condition.

Heidegger's most extended treatment of death is to be found in his greatest work, the massive and complex *Being and Time* [*Sein und Zeit*], first published in 1927. The main target of Heidegger's enquiry is the nature of being, and in particular of human "*Dasein*" (literally "being-there"), a term of art that he defines as follows: "This entity which each of us is himself and which includes inquiring as one of the possibilities of its Being, we shall denote by the term '*Dasein*'" (Heidegger 1962: 27). The reason why Heidegger thinks that a study of death is a crucial component of an investigation of *Dasein* is hinted at in the title to the substantial subsection that deals with the topic: "*Dasein*'s possibility of being-a-whole, and being-towards-death". While *Dasein* lives in the knowledge of its own finitude, Heidegger will argue, the fact that death is not an object of experience must pose a critical obstacle to *Dasein*'s ability to be aware of itself as a whole, since at the instant that its existence has been completed, *Dasein* disappears.

A full unpacking of the multiple meanings that invest Heidegger's pronouncements that our mode of being is being-towards-death, that death is *Dasein*'s "ownmost possibility" and that death "is the possibility of the absolute impossibility of *Dasein*" would require a volume in itself. Fortunately it is possible to extract from Heidegger's rich and intricate text a number of significant theses about death that can be understood and appraised in some degree of isolation from the work's other major themes, even if some of the resonances of Heidegger's discussion may escape us when we so detach it.

If death is not something that we experience, then how can it be a matter of existential concern for us? Heidegger's answer is that death matters to us because we live in its shadow and need to think how best to dispose of the finite amount of time that we have available. It is not enough to characterize human beings as rational and think we have captured their essence, as many earlier philosophers had done. In Heidegger's view, the fact that we are mortal – or, in his own terminology, that our mode of being is *being-towards-death* (*Sein zum Tode*) – is of surpassing importance (*ibid.*: 277). It is crucial that we should take charge of ourselves and live "authentically", that is, decide for ourselves what we shall be and do in the time we have at our disposal, and not allow ourselves to be dominated by what other people expect of us and by social pressures to conform. We need to break free of the stultifying belief that we must do things just because everyone else ("the they [*das Man*]") does them, and in the same way as they do them. If nothing about our acts, judgements, desires and amusements differentiates us from others, then our own *Dasein* is effectively dissolved into "the kind of Being of 'the Others'", and we cease to be "distinguishable and explicit" individuals (*ibid.*: 164).[4] Although thinking about death may make us uncomfortable, it is essential to keep in mind that death impends, and that "*Dasein* cannot outstrip the possibility of death" (*ibid.*: 294).[5] Moreover, it is not just death that cannot be escaped, but the daily necessity to reflect on the practical implications of the fact that our being is being-towards-death.

Since death is inevitable – something "not to be outstripped" – it may at first seem odd that Heidegger constantly refers to it as a "possibility" (*ibid.*: 303). But his meaning is that death, while certain in the long run, is a possible occurrence at any moment. (Jean-Paul Sartre stresses the same thing, referring to death as "the always possible nihilation of my possibles" [1966: 697].) More puzzling is the sense of Heidegger's characterization of death as a person's "ownmost possibility", and the importance that he clearly places on this. To quote him more fully, "death, as the end of *Dasein*, is *Dasein*'s ownmost possibility – non-relational, certain and as such indefinite, not to be outstripped" (Heidegger 1962: 303). Critics have sometimes complained that if the curious adjective "ownmost" (*eigenst*) means something like non-transferable or non-delegatable, then death is not the only thing that can be so described; if no one else can die my death for me, it is also true, as a matter of logic, that no one else can, for example, take on or over my position in the family tree, my virtues, my illness or my reputation. (Another person could consent to face the firing squad instead of me, or take my place at the altar beside the bride I am about to marry, but he would not then die *my* death or contract *my* marriage.) Death does not, therefore, seem to be singled out from many other things when it is labelled "my ownmost possibility".

Sartre is one of Heidegger's critics on this score, arguing that it is only in a trivial sense true that no one but me can die my death, and that "[i]f to die is to die in order to inspire, to bear witness, for the country, *etc.*, then anybody at all can die in my place – as in the song in which lots are drawn to see who is to be eaten" (Sartre 1966: 684). My death, thinks Sartre, does not individualize me, but I must first individualize myself so that I am in a position to make something distinctive of my death, turning it (always provided that it does not take me by surprise) into a "personalized and qualified event", one that expresses my own identity but does not determine it (*ibid.*: 684–5). So while I may make my own death, my death does not make me.

But it is unlikely that Heidegger would wish to deny this. In explaining in what sense human being is being-towards-death, Heidegger does not say that my death, in some obscure way, supplies the principle of my identity, but that in choosing who and what I will be, I need to bear in mind the crucial fact that my existence is temporally limited. Sartre's ascription to Heidegger of the view that my death possesses some mysterious "personalizing virtue" thus appears wide of the mark (*ibid.*: 684). On the latter's account, my death matters to me not *after* it has happened (when I shall be no more), or even *when* it happens, but *before*, during life. By speaking of death as my ownmost possibility, he means to emphasize that my being is being-towards-*my*-death, so that if I am to live authentically I must ensure that I shape and determine that being as fully as lies in my power. That my death is not, from a logical point of view, the only thing that can be described as "my ownmost possibility" is not a problem for Heidegger, since his purpose is to draw attention to the special existential significance of this status in the case of death.

We do not, of course, feel at ease with the thought that we shall die, and we may resort to various strategies to avoid facing up to it. Thus we choose to look on death as something that happens to other people, or we reassuringly tell ourselves that "Death certainly comes, but not right away" (Heidegger 1962: 302). And there is another, more ingenious evasive strategy that we frequently adopt. Instead of refusing to think about our death altogether, we resort to the subtler alternative of looking on our death from a detached and objective point of view, as just another event that will one day occur in the empirical world. In this way, we pretend to take our death seriously when in reality we avoid recognizing death subjectively as our "ownmost possibility", an occurrence of the most fundamental personal concern. As Heidegger puts it, "Dasein is acquainted with death's certainty, and yet evades *Being*-certain" (*ibid.*). This inauthentic approach to death (and therefore life) involves thinking of ourselves as a part of "the They" – the undifferentiated crowd – and failing to recognize the uniquely special meaning that our existence has for us.

It would be a mistake, however, to suppose that living up to Heidegger's ideal of authenticity must preclude all planning for the future on the grounds that one's death might occur at any time. On the contrary, Heidegger advises us to take with maximum seriousness the enterprise of our lives. Indeed, it is just because death is impending that our planning is urgent. In view of the limited number of our days, we need to make the best possible use of them. When we are choosing whether to enlarge our barns, or pursue a career in philosophy, or become a South Seas beachcomber, we must not forget that death – our ownmost, most intimate possibility – will certainly happen, even if we do not know when.[6]

Because death is the outer limit of one's experience and not itself an object of experience, Heidegger draws attention to the fact of *Dasein*'s incapacity to grasp itself as a whole. Although *Dasein* is completed by death, its extinction at the moment of dying means that it can never survey itself in its entirety; what Heidegger calls "everyday *Dasein*" is always only *towards* its end. To recast Heidegger's idea in more everyday language, our view of ourselves is always necessarily incomplete since we cannot estimate the final significance of our lives – their successes and failures, triumphs and tragedies, victories and defeats – until the end; but at *that* very instant, we cease to be (Heidegger 1962: 303). In Heidegger's view, the absolute impossibility of our surveying our lives as wholes is a deeply ironic – even tragi-comic – aspect of *Dasein*.

Yet how important is this inability that Heidegger identifies? It is obviously true that a thing cannot be seen in its entirety before it *is* entire. But how much should this matter to us? If I am in the habit of regularly reviewing my life, I shall one day conduct my final review, when my life is *almost* complete (I may even expire in the very act of retrospection). If I survive to be old, I can be fairly sure, when I then take a comprehensive view of myself, that most of my living has been done. While *Dasein* cannot grasp itself entire, being unable to pass beyond its own limit, it can grasp itself when it is very nearly so. Although Heidegger plainly thinks this existentially unsatisfactory, it is not really clear that he should. In practice, very few thoughtful and reflective people bemoan the fact that they will never be in a position to survey their lives in their absolute totality.

That my death marks my ultimate boundary does, though, have existential significance of another kind, which is gestured towards in a remark of the French novelist and philosopher Simone de Beauvoir. Because "death is the external limit of my possibilities and not a possibility of my own", she notes, I cannot grasp the full meaning of my own mortality from my own experience. Instead, "I know that I am mortal, just as I know that I am old, by adopting the outsider's view of me" (1972: 441). De Beauvoir's talk of my death as "*not* a possibility of my own" may at first seem at odds with Heidegger's description of it as "my ownmost possibility". But de Beauvoir is not really in disagreement with Heidegger here; her point, which Heidegger also stresses, is that once we are dead we have run out of possibilities.

Yet de Beauvoir does take us one step beyond the Heideggerian position. It is a major thesis of *Being and Time* that we only understand death in its true existential significance when we grasp it subjectively, as our ownmost possibility, this being quite different from seeing death in a disengaged objective way, as a fact of everyday empirical experience. When we witness the deaths of others, according to Heidegger, we are at most "just 'there alongside'"; we may feel a sense of loss but "we have no access to the loss-of-Being as such which the dying man 'suffers'" (Heidegger 1962: 282). Ivan Ilych knew that all men were mortal, and that Caius would die, but it took the onset of his own fatal illness to bring him to the anxious awareness of his own being-towards-death.

But there is an element of paradox here. For, as de Beauvoir reminds us, we cannot fully grasp what death means for us by taking the "insider's" point of view alone. We must also bring to bear what we learn from the "outsider's" perspective – the stance we assume towards others' deaths – and apply this to our own case in order that our subjective reflection should be supplied with all relevant data. Subjective insight is therefore not only supplemented by, but also in part dependent on, knowledge from the objective perspective. We know from experience what happens to people who die: that their bodies become utterly unresponsive and quickly start to decay, and that this process is irreversible. Experience also reveals the attitudes and emotions that are associated with death: sadness and a sense of loss, sometimes a feeling of relief that a loved one's suffering is over at last, occasionally guilt or remorse.

Our acquaintance with others' deaths thus alerts us to aspects of the meaning of our own mortality, our Being-towards-death, that we could never learn from our unaided self-reflection. As de Beauvoir says: "[m]y 'mortality' is in no way the object of any close, inward experience. I am not unaware of it; in practical life I take it into account in my plans and my decisions, in so far as I treat myself as an Other: but I do not *feel* it" (*ibid.*).

In order fully to grasp the meaning of our own death, we require empirical information, drawn from our experience of other cases, about the fate of the body, the finality and irreversibility of death, and the feelings and responses of the bereaved. Only by projecting these features on to our own case can we gain a comprehensive insight into what it is to possess being-towards-death.

A defender of Heidegger might object that none of this empirically obtained information really contributes anything to my grasp of the *existential* meaning of my death. My expectation that I shall be mourned by those who love or care for me cannot be integral to my understanding of what my death means *to me*, since it concerns, rather, what my death will mean to others, the bystanders who are merely "there alongside" me. But this line should, I think, be resisted. Part of what my death means to me is constituted by what I understand it will mean to others. It matters immensely to me whether I can expect my passing to be lamented as a sad or celebrated as a happy event. In any case, as we have seen, the interpretation of death is culturally variable and interlocks with a society's view of the world (including its cosmological and theological beliefs) and its ethical ideals. So what I make of my own death is inevitably dependent on how death is understood within my community. If, say, I am persuaded that giving my life in battle for my God or my country or my emperor is the noblest act I can perform and will bring me an eternal reward in paradise, I may actively seek such a death, believing that nothing in my life will become me like the leaving it. If, on the other hand, I think that in dying I shall lose everything there is of value, I will do my best to avoid it for as long as possible (absent any compelling ethical requirement for self-sacrifice).

The focus of existentialist writers on death as my "ownmost possibility" and an event of intimate significance for me has a tendency to obscure the social context in which death occurs. Linnell Secomb has argued in an important article that our relation to the dying is often rather poorly characterized in terms of "bystanding". She proposes that being with others in their dying not only teaches us things about death that we could not otherwise know but has a transforming effect on who we are. Our identities are constructed through our being with others, in their living and their dying:

> [A]gainst Heidegger, I suggest that being-with others *is* constitutive of our being. We only become human in our relations with others: we approach our Being through others, adopting their habits, imitating their techniques of living and being, and also learning modes of dying from them ... I experience "my" death through a process of dwelling-with-death.
>
> (Secomb 1999: 114)[7]

Secomb asserts that she wishes to "augment" rather than contradict Heidegger's account of our relation to death. Nevertheless, the shift in emphasis that she calls for is considerable. To make it is to move to a richer, more realistic view of the relationship between our understanding of our own and of other people's deaths than we find in the pages of *Being and Time*. Despite the incisiveness with which Heidegger describes our anxiety in the face of the death we cannot outstrip and the difficulty of maintaining an authentic, non-evasive awareness that our being is being-towards-death, there hovers about the text that air of "morbid solipsism" that prompts Solomon's complaint that Heidegger omits to see that "I am part of [others'] world as they are part of mine" (1998: 176).[8]

Death, then, is far from being a wholly private affair, of concern only to the decedent. Any death necessitates some greater or lesser reconfiguration of social patterns. People who were close to a deceased person may find their lives profoundly affected by the death and be forced to reconsider the direction of their own being-towards-death. Experiences of the deaths of loved ones are for most people among the most powerful and painful that they ever undergo (the German existentialist writer Karl Jaspers refers to them as "the deepest incision in phenomenal life" [1970: 194]), and major stimulants of existential reflection on the point and meaning of their own lives. And I cannot achieve a full sense of the significance of my own death without reflecting on the impact it will have on others. My death sunders social connections that are intrinsic constituents of my identity (which is not to say that *all* the relationships I am involved in with other people are such; some, obviously, are quite trivial or impersonal). Therefore the meaning that my death has for me cannot be divorced from the meaning that it has for those whom I leave behind.

Death as the completion of life

Dr Johnson's remark that the thought of impending death concentrates the mind wonderfully is reminiscent of Seneca's observation that for many "poor wretches" the close approach of death makes them "realize too late that for all this time they have been preoccupied in doing nothing" (Seneca 2005: 78). Thinking about death may be a stimulant to the wits, but many people (Heidegger would probably say *most*) engage in such reflection too late, or too half-heartedly, for it to have much impact on the way they live. To those who lament the shortness of human life, Seneca makes the uncompromising reply: "It is not that we have a short time to live, but that we waste a lot of it. Life is long enough, and a sufficiently generous amount has been given for the highest achievements if it were all well invested. ... life is long if you know how to use it" (*ibid*.: 59–60). Rightly considered, it is not death that wastes us, but we that waste ourselves.

Seneca recommends that instead of moaning that death takes us before we are ready to go, we should pursue those things (e.g. philosophy) that bring fulfilment and avoid squandering our time on worthless activities and idle amusements. In substance, his advice is similar to Heidegger's: that we should live authentically in the awareness that our being is being-towards-death. Life, says Seneca, is as long as we make it. We should not assume that a man has lived a long life just because he has white hair and wrinkles; it may be that "he has not lived long, just existed long". Life may be compared to a voyage by sea, but some people, Seneca suggests, never get out of the harbour. Someone whose boat has been caught in a raging storm as he left the quayside, and been driven round and round by contrary winds, has not made a long voyage but just endured "a lot of tossing about" (*ibid*.: 67).

Seneca's consolation for mortality may, to be sure, sound rather complacent when we consider that some people die young, before they have had an adequate chance to fulfil their potential. It is sadly *not* always true that "a sufficiently generous amount [of time] has been given for the highest achievements". But Seneca would probably not deny this. His target is, rather, the many people who complain that even a comparatively lengthy lifespan is too short to be satisfying. It is to them that his message is really directed: make the most of your time and opportunities and you will be less likely to feel, at the end, that you still have unfinished business.

A thesis with echoes of Seneca's is to be found in the work of Jaspers. The anticipation of the non-being that is death will horrify us to the extent that we have failed to develop our possibilities in worthwhile ways:

> A realised potential, on the other hand, fulfils my life until old age may permit me to tire of living. ... I feel dread to the extent

to which I failed to live – failed, that is, to make decisions, and
thus come to myself – and I feel at peace insofar as I realised
my potential.   (Jaspers 1970: 199–200)

Too many people, however, fail to rise to the challenge of living
well. Their maxim is "Let us eat and drink, for tomorrow we die"
(1 Corinthians 15:32). For them, life is mere existence – mundane
existence, as Jaspers sometimes calls it – as distinct from "*Existenz*",
by which he designates the individual self that seeks to realize the full-
est human possibilities by the exercise of its own freedom (see *ibid.*:
book II, ch. 1). Jaspers witheringly describes the attitude of those who
are content to follow the crowd, and who mistake for the real joy of
living the frantic pursuit of pleasure, as "a posture of endless, purely
self-exhausting and repetitive enjoyment of unresolved existence"
(*ibid.*: 200). Even when their lives are long in years, they are regret-
tably vacuous in content.

Although *Existenz* clearly needs to take death seriously, Jaspers
candidly concedes that it is hard to maintain, and still harder to
justify, any single attitude to death. In the course of a subtle analysis of the meanings that death has for us, he acknowledges (more
tolerantly than Seneca) that a fear and dislike of death is likely to
be felt even by people whose lives are well spent. We have good
reason to fear death if we suspect that our lives have been unfulfilled (or, as Jaspers puts it, if our existence has been "coupled
with the nonbeing of *Existenz*"), for this is tantamount to a fear
that we have lived "a life without potential, without effect and
communication" (*ibid.*: 199). If we look on life as a party, then
death will inevitably appear as the ultimate party-pooper. But is
it reasonable to be horror-struck in the face of death as "radical
nonbeing"? Jaspers suggests that whether *Existenz* should look
on death as a friend or a foe, shun it or crave it, is a question
with no obviously right answer. In some moods, we think of death
as peace or rest after a busy life. In others, the anticipation of
death fills us with despair, and we "cling to life with every fibre
of [our] being", preferring "any kind of real existence to shadowy
nonbeing". (Such despair may actually be beneficial to us, thinks
Jaspers, since it tends to reinforce our determination to make the
most of our lives, and "[l]ife grows deeper in the face of death"
(*ibid.*).) On the whole, the best plan is to cultivate an attitude of

composure in which both the fear of death and the joy of living are kept before us.

One seemingly attractive way to think about death is as the *completion* of life. Several philosophers have found it fruitful to compare lives to narratives or stories, with a beginning, a middle and an end. So, for instance, John Martin Fischer has observed that, "[i]f our lives are narratives, or have the distinctive structure of narrative, then they must have endings" (2005: 397). In so far as we realize our potential and fulfil our worthwhile aims, death may appear to be the neat conclusion of our story, the last full-stop that ends a well-told and finished tale. But Jaspers doubts whether this is ever how death appears to the subject: "a life may have the character of completeness as a spectacle for others, but it never has that character in reality. Life remains a matter of tensions and goals, inadequate and unfinished" (Jaspers 1970: 200). Some of Jaspers's remarks suggest that he takes it to be an empirical truth that since we continue to form goals and take an active interest in the future to the very end of our lives, we inevitably die with some of our projects unfinished and hopes unfulfilled. While this has some plausibility as a thesis about human psychology, it may be qualified by noting that the older we get the fewer and more circumscribed our projects tend to become; so that much of what we have sought to do in our lifetimes may, with luck, have been achieved by the time we die.

But there are also indications that Jaspers thinks that the notion of completing a life is misconceived in a deeper sense. All lives end, but if we say that a life is "complete" we do not mean simply that it is over but that it has achieved a certain kind of closure. A completed life would be one with no loose ends, unclosed loops or unfinished business. (Strictly speaking, if a life were not complete in this sense then death could not supply what was missing, since nothing can come of nothing; but talk of death "completing" life should be construed as meaning that *when* death comes, life is complete.) But Jaspers adumbrates two reasons for supposing that such completeness is not really possible or, to be more precise, that it is impossible from the point of view of *Existenz*.

The first is that since death is our impassable boundary and the end of the subjective point of view, it offers no vantage point from which we can take a retrospective look at ourselves. So there is never a time at which my life will be complete *for me*. As long as

I live, my business is unfinished, while after my death there is no longer an *I* to conduct an overview. However, two reflections may serve to mitigate the force of this claim. The first (which we have met already in relation to Heidegger's contention that *Dasein* can never grasp itself as a whole) is that while we are never in a position to see our lives literally in their entirety, we can come very close to this when we engage in self-reflection at points close to death. The second is that, if we have reason to believe that death is drawing near, there will normally be steps we can take to conclude or wind down our projects, discharge our responsibilities, pay our debts both literal and metaphorical, and generally make our peace with the world. In this way we can provide our lives with some degree of closure, and know that we have done so, although we may regret the loss of further opportunities that our death will entail. (It is worth noting here the distinction between living a life that is complete in this structural sense and living a complete human lifespan of seventy or eighty years. People who are cut off in their prime may achieve the former without the latter, although many also achieve the latter without the former.)

The second, and quite different, reason that Jaspers offers for thinking the idea of completing a life misguided is presented in a disconcerting trio of sentences: "In life our every achievement is like a corpse. Nothing finished can live. In pursuit of completion we seek something that is finished and thus dead" (Jaspers 1970: 200). Jaspers does little to elucidate these rather obscure remarks, but their thrust is presumably that a project that is completed ceases to be a focus of attention and activity and becomes a matter of record rather than of current concern. Whatever importance it may formerly have had is lost once other enterprises have displaced it. Not even a project's successful completion is sufficient to make it of abiding interest. Finished things are a part of the past, inert and corpselike. And what goes for individual projects goes likewise for whole lives. A completed life would be one that no longer possessed any existential importance and would, indeed, be no better than death. In the self-destructiveness of such completion, *Existenz* itself (which, according to Jaspers, cannot survive "without potential, without effect and communication") would have ceased to be. Thus we arrive again at the conclusion that it is impossible for a life to be complete from the point of view of *Existenz*.

This argument, I believe, purveys an overly gloomy view of the value of human enterprise and achievement. In fact Jaspers's remarks would seem to imply an even more pessimistic position than he explicitly states, for if nothing we do has any lasting value, it is not at all clear why we should go to the trouble of doing it in the first place. Jaspers might respond to this that the things we do are valuable at the time we do them – that it is the journey rather than the arrival that matters. But what could make the journey worthwhile if its outcome were a matter of indifference? The only obvious answer seems to be the pleasure that we take in it. But for Jaspers to make this reply would be to undermine his own thesis that to centre our lives on pleasure is to adopt a "posture of endless, purely self-exhausting and repetitive enjoyment of unresolved existence".

Jaspers's remarks on the transient value of our activities resemble those of another pessimistic commentator on human affairs, Richard Taylor. According to this author, nothing that we do has ultimately any more point than the labours of Sisyphus, who in Greek myth was condemned by the gods, as a punishment for betraying their secrets, to roll a heavy stone up a steep hill, repeatedly and for ever.

> Our achievements, even though they are often beautiful, are mostly bubbles; and those that do last, like the sand-swept pyramids, soon become mere curiosities while around them the rest of mankind continues its perpetual toting of rocks, only to see them roll down. Nations are built upon the bones of their founders and pioneers, but only to decay and crumble before long, their rubble then becoming the foundation of others directed to exactly the same fate.   (Taylor 1984: 263)[9]

But this is a travesty of the truth. Here are just a few examples of human achievements, ancient and modern, that have not merely escaped oblivion but have had a permanent and transformative effect on what has come after them: the *Iliad*, the Parthenon, the Christian gospel, Roman law, polyphony, Chartres Cathedral, the *Divine Comedy*, printing from movable type, the banking system, *Hamlet*, Raphael's Vatican frescoes, Bach's Mass in B minor, vaccination, motive power, Kant's *Critique of Pure Reason*, the special theory of relativity, penicillin, radio, the microchip. Besides such public accomplishments, there are all the private and personal projects and achievements that enrich the lives of individuals and of the people around them. If one takes a degree, brings up a child, learns to play the violin, assists a friend through a phase of depression or raises money for famine relief, the effects of what one does may be far-reaching and long-lasting. As things that make a difference, these are neither bubbles nor "mere curiosities".

It might be contended on Jaspers's behalf that achievements with enduring effects are not, in his sense, "finished", and that it is only those that are of no further significance and quickly forgotten that merit being labelled "dead". This kindly interpretation, however, is hard to sustain. It is doubtful, for one thing, whether we could properly describe something as an "achievement" if it had no abiding effects on anyone or anything. There is also the evidence of the text itself: "[i]n life", writes Jaspers, "our *every* achievement is a corpse" (*ibid.*, emphasis added). Jaspers appears radically to underestimate the extent to which many of our projects and enterprises influence the shape of things to come, and resonate in many other lives. (Consider, for instance, how profoundly such a natural and common "enterprise" as having children affects the human future.) Moreover, our own efforts interlock with those of other people in complex patterns of agency that do not come to an end as soon as we do. In fact, apart from very trivial things, there is little that we do that ever becomes "purely past".

What is true of particular projects is true also of life as a whole. All of us influence the future in multiple ways. And this is perhaps a comforting thought, making death seem less final and destructive. At the same time, we can hope that our lives will attain completeness in the different sense that death will not strike us down in the middle of things, before we have brought our projects to a suitable degree of fruition. The kind of closure we seek does not always require that we should bring our major projects to their ultimate conclusion. It is enough for us to be able to feel that we have "done our bit" in regard to them, and can confidently hope that others will now do theirs. Like runners in a relay race, we can hand the baton on to our team-mates when we have run our stage. It may be objected to this that it is hard to see how I can accord any importance to what will happen to my projects after my death, when my own subjectivity is extinct. But there is really no good reason why

I should not count among the things that give my life meaning and value now, the fact that the projects I have been engaged with will have meaning and value for others when I am gone.

Before we leave the subject of death as the completion of life, it is worth glancing briefly at the so-called *Liebestod* (literally, "love's death") tradition of German romanticism, which, in the crisp characterization of David Cooper, sees death as "the triumphant 'perfection' of the drab business of living" (1999: 134). This tradition reaches its acme and receives its definitive statement in Richard Wagner's opera *Tristan und Isolde*, where the two lovers, in an ecstatic encounter, sing of their longing for death, which they portray as a blessed night in which their love will be forever uninterrupted by the inane distractions of the day. The attraction of death, in the *Liebestod* tradition, is that it permits a radical simplification of existence, allowing us the opportunity to strip life down to its essentials. In existentialist language, death affords the prospect of a more authentic – because less cluttered and random – existence than is possible during life. He who has once lovingly looked on death's night, says Tristan, "has one only longing, a longing for the holy night where forever, solely true, love and rapture wait". Isolde's response is to wish that the night of love will make her forget that she lives, and the pair then sing together of their desire to be free of the world and its vanities by falling into a sleep from which they shall never waken (*Tristan und Isolde* II.ii; Wagner 1965: 17–18).

Despite the sublimity of Wagner's music and poetry, which lends these sentiments conviction while one listens, it is not easy in the cold light of day – if we may adopt so profane a stance – to take them very seriously. Even Isolde has her momentary doubts, asking Tristan: "Would not day and death as equals overtake our love and rend it?" Tristan's answer, that their love is too powerful to be annihilated by death,[10] actually undermines rather than upholds the *Liebestod* theme, by conceding that death destroys rather than fulfils, and that if their love survives it will do so in spite of death and not because of it. In any case, Tristan's confidence that their love is everlasting relies heavily on the assumption that death is not the end of us, and that some kind of subjective experience is possible after death. If that assumption is rejected, then the *Liebestod* idea must be rejected along with it. But even if we believed that there was life after death, how could we be sure that our afterlife would be focused on those themes and elements that were most important to us in our earthly lives? Would Tristan and Isolde's love survive death, and would the bodiless pair still exert the strong attraction on each other that they previously did as embodied persons? (Maybe like those other ghostly lovers Rafi and Pervaneh they would soon forget each other.) How can we know what it would mean to live authentically in a purely spiritual or immaterial world (presuming that such would be the setting for the afterlife), which is quite beyond anything in our present experience?

It is unnecessary to pursue these irresolvable speculations. A more pertinent observation is that the *Liebestod* idea may rest to some extent on a simple conflation of a false thesis with a true one. The true claim is that some lives are improved ("perfected" may be too strong a word) by the manner of their dying. The treacherous Thane of Cawdor in *Macbeth* made up for some of his past delinquencies by dying bravely: "Nothing in his life/ Became him like the leaving it" (I.iv.7–8). In Dickens's *A Tale of Two Cities*, Sydney Carton redeems his wasted life by dying on the guillotine in place of the husband of the woman he loves. Wittgenstein described his father's death as a "beautiful" death, one "worth a whole life" (in Cooper 1999: 134).[11] Many ordinary people exhibit a notable patience and fortitude when dying from painful and distressing conditions such as cancer. In all these cases, lives come not just to a close but achieve a kind of closure that enhances their value. But this is quite different from saying that lives can find fulfilment *in*, or after, death. This claim could only be true if we survived our bodily death in a state that permitted some form of existentially satisfying existence to continue, and that, I argued in Chapter 1, is highly improbable. While we can die well, we cannot be well when dead.

In her account of the last illness and death of her mother, de Beauvoir remarks, in what amounts to the antithesis of the *Liebestod* thesis, that "All men must die: but for every man his death is an accident and, even if he knows it and consents to it, an unjustifiable violation". Even when a person dies honourably and virtuously, death is not the opening to a brave new world but an event "as violent and unforeseen as an engine stopping in the middle of the sky" (de Beauvoir 1969: 92). The sense in which our being is being-towards-death is not that articulated by Tristan, and while our lives may or may not be drab we cannot hope to improve on them by dying.

3 Long lives, short lives

How long should we live?

In one of his *Dialogues of the Dead*, the Greek satirist Lucian of Samosata presents a conversation in Hades between the Cynic philosopher Menippus and the centaur Chiron, who had voluntarily relinquished his immortality. What, asks Menippus, had made Chiron so fond of death, a thing that most people shun? Was it not very pleasant to be alive and to see the light of day? But Chiron retorts that you can have too much of a good thing:

> I consider pleasure to come from variety and change; but I was living on and on, and enjoying the same things – sun, light and food; the seasons were always the same, and everything came in its turn, one thing seeming to follow automatically upon another; and so I had too much of it all, for I found my pleasure not in always having the same thing, but also in doing quite without it. (Lucian 1961: 41, 43)

Although Chiron is so far enjoying the contrasting conditions to be found in the underworld, Menippus sows a doubt in his mind. Won't life here too, he asks, become equally monotonous in the course of time? When Chiron asks anxiously whether there is anything that can be done to avoid this, the philosopher replies that one should do what a sensible man does: "be content and satisfied with one's lot and think no part of it intolerable" (ibid.: 43, 45).

A cynical response to this response of the Cynic would be to point out that this might be more easily said than done. One could try one's best to be satisfied with one's lot but find it increasingly hard with the passage of the centuries. Contentment is not, unfortunately, a condition under the direct control of the will. However, the question whether a life that never ended would be eternally tedious may seem to be of only hypothetical importance unless we believe that there is personal survival of death. But this appearance is deceptive, since even if we reject the idea of an afterlife, thinking about the question can help us to make up our minds whether to look on death as a curse or a blessing. On the face of it, the longer we live, the better, since more time means more opportunity to enjoy the good things of life – hence Menippus's remark that death is "a thing for which most men have no love". But this presupposes that we would continue to find life pleasant and fulfilling even if it went on for ever, and there are solid reasons for doubting this. Some philosophers have urged that eternal existence would not only be boring but would induce in us a deep sense of absurdity, since we would be confronted (as Chiron notes) with the prospect of endlessly repeating the same experiences. Perhaps, as Bernard Williams (1973b) has suggested, we should look on death not as a destroyer of meaningful life but as a crucial condition of our lives having meaning.

Boredom sets in, thinks Charles Hartshorne, when the proper balance between novelty and repetition, which is the basis for all our zest in living, becomes upset in favour of repetition. Old animals and old people are bored animals and bored people because they have "felt and done most of the things that must be felt and done so many times before". Hartshorne quotes the elderly Thomas Jefferson, who wrote in a letter to a friend, "I am tired of putting my clothes on every morning and taking them off every evening" (Hartshorne 1958: 387). When we are old and losing our zest death is a good thing, thinks Hartshorne, because it spares us from an otherwise inevitable descent into a state of tedium.

Walter Kaufmann goes so far as to claim that "[f]or most of us death does not come soon enough". Short lives, he suggests, have a special intensity about them that long ones do not, and "[l]ives are spoiled and made rotten by the sense that death is distant and irrelevant". In a reminiscence of the *Liebestod* idea, Kaufmann maintains that not only love but "all life" is enriched by the expectation of death – the more so where one has reason to anticipate an early "rendezvous with death" (1963: 373). A person lives better and more vitally if he expects to live for only thirty or forty years rather than survive into dreary decrepitude.

These views – even the more moderate ones of Hartshorne – are, to say the least, open to question. Many people are at their most zestful and enthusiastic in youth, but that is hardly a good reason for supposing that it would be best for them to die while they are still in their prime of life. In any case, even when the balance between novelty and repetition is set firmly in favour of novelty, novelty is not always pleasant, particularly when it has to be faced with relative inexperience. Youth is not a period of unalloyed happiness for most people, and many of the emotional, social and economic problems of the young find their resolution only in middle age (the trials of youth are, of course, the theme in countless popular novels of the *Bildungsroman* genre). Every phase of a human lifespan offers its own challenges and opportunities and even old age brings new experiences, both pleasant and unpleasant (e.g. enjoying seeing our grandchildren grow up, or learning to cope with failing health and strength).

Corliss Lamont, taking issue with Hartshorne's assertion that old people are generally bored people, reminds us that there are a great many who are not. And even those who are need not be, since there are always new books to read, new sights to see and new things to do to ensure that life remains interesting. He also challenges the claim that repetition is always tedious. Such activities as drinking pure water, making love, listening to a great symphony or viewing one's favourite natural vistas of forest or mountain, he suggests, continue to be satisfying however often we do them. Because there are many things we do that "can be carried on in patterns of variety that seldom give rise to monotony", Lamont concludes that he would "rejoice in living on as an immortal upon our earth or in some other place equally attractive" (1965: 32–3).[1]

There is, though, a big difference – indeed, an infinite one – between living a very long life and living for ever. Lamont might enjoy skiing down his favourite snow-covered slope in Vermont at the age of 100 (if he were still capable), or 200, but can he be sure that he would still enjoy it if he were 10,000 or a million years old, or if his years were past counting? Since no human being has ever lived much beyond a century, we can only speculate on what it would feel like to live a *really* long life. Probably much would turn on what one had done with one's life, and how creatively one had developed and utilized one's opportunities. Someone of Lamont's temperament might well make a greater success of serious longevity than would the fifty-year-old man who once told me that he had now done everything he wished to do and was ready to die. Yet, as we shall see in the next section, there are some persuasive reasons for thinking that, however much enthusiasm and resourcefulness one brought to the business of living, one would find it very hard to retain a sense of one's identity *and* continue to find life fulfilling if one were immortal.

Lamont describes his own liking for the idea of immortality as arising from "a profound sense of the sweetness and splendor of life". However, he also, without seeming to notice the tension, ascribes his sentiments to "the innate urge for self-preservation" (Lamont 1965: 33). This combination is problematic, since a basic instinct to continue living and stave off death for as long as possible has little to do with any positive, self-conscious valuation of life and its possibilities. Members of quite lowly animal species have a powerful instinct for self-preservation but we would not attribute to them the thought that death is bad because life is beautiful. And we are all familiar with instances of people whose lives have become very painful and unhappy yet in whom the urge for self-preservation is undiminished. So we cannot infer from the existence in us of a strong instinct for self-preservation that life without end would be good for us. That we are naturally disposed to flee death is not a proof that death could never be a blessing.

In his book *The Tragic Sense of Life in Men and in Peoples* ([1912] 1931), the Spanish author Miguel de Unamuno voiced one of the most powerful laments for the inevitability of death to be found in modern literature. Conceding that arguments for the immortality of the soul were, on the most favourable estimation, inconclusive, Unamuno nonetheless found himself unable to accept the horrifying idea that bodily death might be the end of us. That I who am "the centre of my universe, the centre of the universe" should expire is so unendurable a thought, according to Unamuno, that the heart is entitled to overrule reason and reject it. While in Unamuno's view the "immortal yearning for immortality" (1931: 38) lies deep within the soul of all human beings, it is hard to avoid the impression that he himself felt this longing with an intensity that bordered on the hysterical:

> I do not want to die – no; I neither want to die nor do I want to want to die; I want to live for ever and ever and ever. I want this "I" to live – this poor "I" that I am and that I feel myself to be here and now, and therefore the problem of the duration of my soul, of my own soul, tortures me. (1931: 45)[2]

Unamuno's passionate hatred of death is ostensibly provoked by his sense of what we lose by dying (if death is the end of us): nothing less than the whole universe. This attitude, he admits, is grounded on egoism, which he sees as "the principle of psychic gravity, the necessary postulate" of human existence (*ibid.*: 45–6). There is an unmistakable echo of Wittgenstein in his talk of my losing at my death a world that is at once *my* world and *the* world. Yet we might suspect that it is the natural instinct for self-preservation rather than any rationalization that is at the root of Unamuno's lament for mortality. He remarks that if someone were to ask him why he wanted to be immortal, he would reply that he did not understand the question. The less than perspicuous gloss he provides on this response – that posing such a question would be asking "the reason of the reason, the end of the end, the principle of the principle" – appears to be saying that the desire for survival is too fundamental a part of our make-up to need or admit of justification. There is no point in asking whether we *ought* to desire immortality if we cannot help but do so.

But it is far from evident that we have any innate desire for immortality, as distinct from an instinct for self-preservation. If human beings lived immensely longer than they actually do, this instinct might still kick in and make us feel uncomfortable at the approach of death. Nevertheless, if we had lived long enough to be wearied by the prospect of further living, we might rationally consider our dying to be a welcome release. Any desire for immortality is more likely to be a product of philosophic reflection on the existential predicament than a gut feeling induced by natural evolution. Besides, it is hard to see what evolutionary advantages would stem from our developing such a desire, when genetic and species health is better served by the regular replacement of individuals than by their prolonged survival.

It is possible to regret, with Unamuno, the fact of human transience without believing that nothing short of immortality would do for us. It is true that even eighty or a hundred years are only a drop in the ocean of eternity, and part of what moves Unamuno and others who feel like him may be the egoistic dislike not just of ceasing to be, but of ceasing to make an impact on posthumous ages.[3] Even if we and our works are remembered for a time after our deaths, this situation will not last for ever. But should this really bother us? Thomas Nagel (1979c: 11) notes that if nothing we do now will matter in a million years, by the same token what will matter (or not) in a million years should not be of any concern to us now. In any case, our natural constitution does not equip us to make an impact on eternity and it is hard to believe that our good could really lie in something for which we were so ill-designed.

Yet there surely is something that we may rationally regret about human lives as they are. To anticipate a claim that I shall discuss more fully in a later chapter, a problem with our actual lives is that they are frequently too short for us to have time to realize fully all the investments we have made in them. A lifespan of (say) 200 or 300 years is a long way short of eternity. But – and despite what Seneca says about most lives being long enough – many people could probably make good use of those extra years, and lead a life that was not only fuller in content but more satisfactory in structure than our lives are now. Much that we presently do is done hurriedly, or is left rude and unfinished; "time's wingèd chariot" is always travelling too fast for comfort. We feel frustrated by our lack of opportunity to develop ourselves in new ways, or fully enough in old ones. We are compelled to make painful choices between attractive courses of action and lifestyles, knowing that we cannot do everything. Should we become a philosopher or a footballer, a concert pianist or a world-traveller? If we had an extra century or two, we could be them all.

It is one of the ironies of human existence that although we have evolved into sophisticated creatures capable of a vast repertoire of complex behaviours, the shortness of our lives prevents our making use of more than a fraction of our potential. Even the longest of lives is telescoped towards the point of absurdity. Projects crowd in on us but only a few can engage our serious attention, and even these can prove frustrating. We spend years in developing our mastery of novel-writing or tennis-playing or transplant surgery, only to find that we no sooner reach our peak than we begin to decline from it. *Si jeunesse savait, si vieillesse pouvait*:[4] decrepitude sets in before we are able to make the most of the talents for living we have so slowly (and painfully) acquired in our youth. Think how different our situation would be if we retained the mind and body of a healthy thirty- or forty-year-old for a hundred years or so. (We would also have more time to repair our significant mistakes.) Eighty or ninety years may be a comparatively long lifespan as actual lives go, but it is woefully inadequate for the realization of a person's full potential. Someone who lives to 90 at least completes the curve that leads from infancy through maturity to old age and death; yet the curve is pathetically short.

The tedium of immortality?

Chiron, we saw, thought that we can have too much of life. The same message is vividly conveyed in Jorge Luis Borges's story "The Immortal" (1970), which describes the quest by a Roman legionary tribune for a fabled city inhabited by a race who have drunk from the river of immortality. When the searcher, after years of frightful hardships and dangers, finally lights upon the immortals, he fails at first to recognize them in a tribe of silent and isolated troglodytes who subsist on the flesh of serpents. In time he manages to extract their story from one of them, whom he encourages to speak for the first time in centuries (in a further twist, which we need not explore, this man turns out to be the poet Homer). The tribune learns that the immortals had long since become bored with the repetitiveness of life in their fine city and had razed it to the ground, replacing it with a labyrinthine and irrational city, full of dead-end corridors, upside-down stairways and uninhabitable houses. Following the completion of this bitter joke, they had retired to dwell in caves, where they tried to forget the physical world and lose themselves in pure speculation. While this might seem *prima facie*, to a philosophical audience, a fairly attractive career move, it is made clear that the troglodytes' state is not to be envied. Having mostly forgotten how to speak, they have reverted to a bestial, semi-demented condition and lost all interest in their own fate. Their pure thought has degenerated into mere trance. In a sense that is more than just metaphorical, they have largely lost themselves.

We do not need to accept Borges's fantasy as an especially plausible account of counterfactual psychology: of how people would be likely to respond if they found themselves unable to age or die. (In particular the immortals' withdrawal from social life into an eremitical existence where thinking is the sole activity seems an outstandingly inapt strategy for beating boredom.) Borges's intention is not to write realistically but to dramatize what he sees as some important truths about the human situation. In radical contrast to Unamuno, Borges believes that immortality would be a curse of the first magnitude, and that if we lived endless lives we would be doomed to a joyless, absurd and intolerable existence from which the only ultimate escape would be dementia.

The passage in which the tribune narrator sums up the nature of the immortals' tragedy is worth quoting at length:

> Death (or its allusion) makes men precious and pathetic. They are moving because of their phantom condition; every act they execute may be their last; there is not a face that is not on the verge of dissolving like a face in a dream. Everything among the mortals has the value of the irretrievable and the perilous. Among the Immortals, on the other hand, every act (and every thought) is the echo of others that preceded it in the past, with no visible beginning, or the faithful presage of others that in the future will repeat it to a vertiginous degree. There is nothing that is not as if lost in a maze of indefatigable mirrors. Nothing can happen only once, nothing is preciously precarious. The elegiacal, the serious, the ceremonial, do not hold for the Immortals. (Borges 1970: 146)

Three distinct costs of living for ever are identified in this passage. The first is that fragile and passing things are valued at a premium by us, since we know they will not always be there and that we must make the most of them while they are; and this applies also to finite human lives. If I were to live for ever, my life and all it contains would lose this preciousness in both my own and other people's eyes. Secondly, immortality would involve the mind-numbing repetition of acts and experiences, and the extinction of all sense of novelty. There would be nothing new for us under the sun and no reason to value our time, since anything we could do today might safely be deferred indefinitely.

Thirdly, and most originally, Borges hints that the aesthetic modes in which we respond creatively to our experience, and by doing so deepen and enrich it, would be out of place in a world of immortals. In part, this is connected with the first cost, as the preciousness of the transient has always been among the greatest inspirations of poetry and art. The knowledge that we may lose what we love makes us love it the more, and the attachments that we form, which are commonly shot through with a vein of melancholy, seek expression not only in art strictly so called but also in religious practices and philosophical reflection. Since everyone and everything that we care about is fated, as Shakespeare says, to be "by Time's fell hand defaced" (Sonnet 64), we have ample motive to celebrate present joys and lament past ones. We may also be moved to fix the emotions of the moment in ways that prolong them beyond the life of their objects, as Shakespeare did when he penned the "powerful rhyme" that would preserve the memory of his love "'Gainst death and all oblivious enmity" (Sonnet 55).[5]

A similar conclusion to Borges's – that immortality would be bad for us – is reached in a much-discussed paper by Bernard Williams. In "The Makropulos Case: Reflections on the Tedium of Immortality" (1973b), Williams takes his cue from a play by Karel Čapek (best known nowadays in Leoš Janáček's operatic version), which tells the story of a woman who had been given the recipe of the elixir of life in her youth, and who, when the action opens, has attained the age of 342. This woman, known as Elina Makropulos (and formerly by a variety of other names, all with the initials "EM"), is profoundly bored by an existence that offers no fresh experiences, and she has become indifferent to all the standard satisfactions of human life. Seeing no escape from the tedium of living, she finally chooses not to take the elixir any more and dies. In Williams's view, she does the right thing.

What would have to be the case for immortality to be attractive to us? Williams proposes two individually necessary and jointly sufficient conditions. First, our personal identity must be preserved throughout that existence. This condition is plausible because if our identity were to change over the course of time then it could not be said that *we* were living for ever; this would not be immortality but a process of replacement of old selves with new. Secondly, for me to find immortality appealing – to quote Williams's own words – "the state in which I survive should be one which, to me looking forward, will be adequately related, in the life it presents, to those aims which I now have in wanting to survive at all" (1973b: 91). While Williams allows that this condition is hard to formulate precisely, he insists that something like it is required, since we are "propelled into the future" by the desires that we actually have or that we can expect to have or envisage having if we retain our present character (*ibid*.: 91–2). I want to see tomorrow, and many more morrows, because I have desires *now* that I hope to see fulfilled *then*. But in Elina Makropulos's case, the forward trajectory of desire has come to a stop. Given the character that she has, she has no more desires, nor any expectation of forming any, that propel her towards the future.

Both of Williams's conditions have been challenged. The point is frequently made that in a situation so counterfactual as one in which we lived for ever, a great many things would presumably be different from the way they are now, and among these things might be certain alterations to human psychology that made us immune to, or better able to deal with, the kind of boredom felt by Elina Makropulos or Borges's immortals. If immortality came naturally, and not, as with Elina, out of a bottle, then nature might also have equipped us with the capacity to enjoy a never-ending life. So perhaps what we should be regretting is not that we are not immortal, but that we are not immortal *and* constructed in such a way that we could maintain our zest throughout an infinite existence. Williams's second condition maintains that we can only look forward to a future that appears desirable to us given the character we now have. This is not meant to exclude our having desires to change aspects of our present character that dissatisfy us: for instance, I might actively seek to develop some extra virtues or rid myself of my vices; yet these projects remain expressions of my existing character. But some writers have suggested that we could look favourably on a future in which we foresaw our character undergoing far more substantial changes, provided that those changes happened very gradually. On this view, if I envisaged that in a thousand years' time I would have an utterly different personality from the one I now have, with a completely different set of desires and interests, I could still prefer to go forwards into that future rather than to die before I arrived there, so long as my progression from here to there involved no radical discontinuities or inexplicable "jumps". Although there may be little or no psychological resemblance between me now and me then, at each stage in my development I have good reason to wish to live until the next stage; and the transformations I undergo will ensure that I am in no danger of becoming stuck in the kind of rut that makes Elina's existence unbearable to her.[6]

One might counter on Williams's behalf that, regardless of the gradual nature of the psychological evolution envisaged on this view, we would have very little reason for desiring *now* to become the very alien creature we anticipate being a thousand years hence. (We might not even *like* the person we foresee or fear ourselves turning into, or want the world to contain people of that kind.) However, McMahan has argued that this, while true, is not an adequate basis for concluding that immortality on such terms would be bad. For at any point in one's career, one "would *then* have a strong time-relative interest in continuing to live beyond that point". Moreover, and crucially, "one has some interest now in assuring the satisfaction of the interests one would have then" (McMahan 2002: 102). An immortal with a character that gradually evolved would always have a rational interest in living for a further considerable time, and (unless the conditions of life were to become intolerable) death would always be unwelcome. Foreseeing this, we would now have, were such a thing possible, a reason for wishing to live for ever.

If McMahan is right, not only can Williams's second condition be dismissed as misguided but the first, too, can be seen to be unimportant. Although McMahan himself does not draw this conclusion explicitly, whether or not the identity of the self would be preserved through the course of radical psychological changes of the kind at issue should be a matter of indifference if the right kind of psychological continuity were to hold throughout the developmental process.[7] Even if it were not strictly *I* who would be living in a thousand years' time, it would be a successor-self whose psychological history led directly back to me and who therefore would stand in a completely different, and much more intimate relation, to me than any other people who were alive at that time (including my own genetic descendants, in whose welfare I may also feel a present interest). Derek Parfit (1984: pt. 3) has famously questioned whether strict personal identity is preserved even within a single (normal) lifespan in view of the profound psychological changes that take place in us between the cradle and the grave. On the Parfitean model, the unity of a human biography is constituted by its psychological continuity, rather than by its being the history of a numerically identical subject from start to finish; it is also entirely rational for us to be concerned about the fate of our successor-selves.

But is McMahan right? We can grant the plausibility of his claim that "an immortal with a gradually evolving character would always, at any given moment, have a strong time-relative interest in continuing to live for a further considerable time (assuming, of course, that his life would be worth living)" (McMahan 2002: 103), but it does not follow from this claim that I have, from my present vantage point, an egoistic reason to desire such a career.

There are two grounds for disagreement with McMahan. First, there are certain kinds of person I should never want to be. But can I safely assume that I shall never, however long I (or my successor-selves) survive, develop a personality like that of Hitler or Jack the Ripper? If I am to avoid tedium for eternity, it would seem that I must in time run through a great many of the possible ways of being human. Borges's narrator remarks: "Homer composed the *Odyssey*; if we postulate an infinite period of time, the impossible thing is not to compose the *Odyssey*, at least once. No one is anyone, one single immortal man is all men" (Borges 1970: 145). This is probably an exaggeration; there seems no reason why we should fill every conceivable human groove even in an infinite existence; but we would undoubtedly fill a very great number. There is a good chance that Dr Jekyll would eventually turn into Mr Hyde, even without the use of a drug. And so too might every other immortal. Not only is such a prospect morally alarming but we could take little satisfaction in being a person of a particular kind if we foresaw that in time we might be a person of a completely opposite kind, and that everyone else was subject to the same transformations, thus further weakening our sense of our own distinctiveness and value.

Secondly, an unending life would be one that lacked any meaningful shape or pattern. It would resemble an infinitely long river that meandered eternally without ever reaching the sea. There would be no arch-shaped structure of birth, growth, maturity, decline and death. Although phases of the life might have their own internal structure, it would be as a whole (not that it could ever be grasped that way) completely shapeless. It would be a life that was going nowhere specific, and in which the people, projects and aspirations that were important at one stage would be insignificant and forgotten at another. On Parfit's view of personal identity, we are capable of taking an intense personal interest in our successor-selves. But it is not credible that such concern could be extended indefinitely far into the future, to successor-selves who were psychologically quite different from us and whose concerns had nothing in common with ours (and might even be antithetical to them).

Furthermore, if we lived for ever we would need to be equipped with vastly more powerful memories than we have now to be able to recall our own distant pasts. McMahan might contend that it would not be important to be able to remember our origins or ancient history so long as we could remember our more recent past (say, the last century or so). But if we retained anything like our present psychology, we would feel ourselves deeply alienated from our own pasts if we had to consult the history books to learn about our former deeds. (Also think what an unsatisfactory sense of self one would have if one could no longer remember one's childhood or one's parents.) We care about what will happen to us in the future, and what happened to us in the past, because we see our past and our future as parts of one and the same life, chapters in the same narrative.[8] No coherent, graspable narrative, however, could link together our existence over endless ages. Fischer has suggested that while an infinitely long life would not have "narrative structure, strictly conceived", the "literary analogue for such a life is not the novel, but perhaps a collection of short stories … with the same character appearing as the protagonist" (2005: 398). But on the model of immortality envisaged, the identity of the character changes along with the plotline. That being so, the attractions of prolonged life on such terms seem nugatory. To speak for myself, I would have little taste for an existence that was, to put it crudely, merely one damn thing after another.

There are thus good reasons to agree with Williams that immortality could not be made attractive to us. This is not to say that there could not be other kinds of beings for which immortality would be tolerable. My guess is that they would have to be either much duller than we are (an immortal sheep or rabbit might never get bored) or more godlike, possessing infinite patience and tranquillity of spirit (although this condition too might be rather hard to distinguish from dullness). Immortality for a sheep or a god may be a good for the subject if the measure of that goodness is the pleasure of the present moment. But neither, with a life extended to eternity, would be able to reap any existential satisfaction from the thought that its life was going somewhere: that it had a goal or *telos*. If we see our ability to think such a thought as a condition of our having a life worth living, then we should not wish for immortality. Death damages the meaningfulness of our lives when it cuts us off in the middle of our projects, making our best efforts futile, or when it deprives us of the chance to realize our full potential. But we should not infer from the contingent fact that death normally occurs too soon that death is necessarily a destroyer of meaning. We could only establish *that* conclusion if we could delineate, as we have not yet, an existentially fulfilling form of immortality.[9]

The alleged antinomy of death

If immortality would be bad for us, then death, provided that its timing is right, should be good for us. The proviso, however, is all-important, and unfortunately it is rarely, if ever, satisfied. For most, maybe for all, of us, death arrives before we have fully done with living.

It is this fact that underlies our sense that death is inevitably and invariably tragic, even where it brings an end to a painful or unhappy condition, for in that case death is still a poor second-best to continued life without the problematic condition. From the first-person point of view, my death is the cancellation of all my possible goods (cf. Nagel 1979b: 9–10). From a third-person viewpoint, when a person dies, something of great value and of unexhausted potential is lost to the world; and while other people will be born, *that* person is gone for good. Ronald Dworkin speaks of a human being as "a masterpiece of nature" (1993: 82), and reminds us of Shakespeare's resounding line, "What a piece of work is a man!" (*Hamlet* II.ii.115). (It is true that many men do their best to spoil nature's handiwork, but it is quite difficult to damage a life so thoroughly that it becomes entirely irredeemable.) At the same time, we are not well suited psychologically to live for ever. It has been suggested that there is a tension between these two thoughts. Immortality would be bad for us yet death, whenever it occurs, means the end of a valuable existence (valuable, at least, for the potential for good it contains). Seemingly, then, death would always be bad, even when it was good. Loptson writes that the two strands of reflection "combine to produce a kind of antinomy: they box the attempt to understand the significance of death into a kind of corner from which no adequate emergence seems possible" (1998: 135). While natural selection has produced on earth "a species of what we may almost call demi-gods", it has "coupled this with the condition of an extremely severe finitude". In Loptson's view, "It is a kind of cosmic rotten trick" (*ibid.*: 150).

How genuine is this "antinomy of death"? To answer this, we must first note some confusion in Loptson's account. In justifying his claim that we have been played "a cosmic rotten trick", Loptson sometimes refers to the inevitability of death and sometimes to the regrettable brevity of our lives. But these should be carefully distinguished. We can quite consistently hold *both* that the grim reaper generally gathers us too early *and* that a life that went on interminably would be bad for us. This is precisely the position that I have defended in this chapter. Loptson is right to associate the misfortune of our early deaths with our evolution into quasi-divine beings of vast ability and potential. "So much to do, so little time to do it" could be the watchword of our species. It *is* a rotten fate to have developed the mental capacity to form spacious ambitions without the physical staying power that would enable us fully to carry them out. But there is no antinomy here. We are not committed to saying that death both is and is not good for us. What is bad is early death (of which we are all the victims), not death *tout court*.

However, Loptson would probably complain that this response misses the main point. The death of any human being is the end of a masterpiece of nature, whether it comes early or late. Even if we lived much longer than we actually do and had the time to realize our potential much more fully, our death would still remove a quasi-demigod from the world. And since death would always have this negative aspect, regardless of how long our lives were *or whether we had done with living*, there is no eliminating the antinomy of death, which appears when we juxtapose two disparate perspectives on value. Elina Makropulos, aged 342, may have had her own good reasons for wanting to die, but her refusal to take any more of the elixir meant that a precious and irreplaceable being would be lost to the world.

There is no reason, of course, to expect that first-person and third-person perspectives on value should always coincide. My good may not be the world's good, and *vice versa*. There is nothing very surprising about this, and we would not normally dignify a clash between my interests and broader public interests in terms of "antinomy" or contradiction. It is not difficult to conceive how a continuation of Elina's life might be better for other people than for herself. Yet just as others may see and value Elina not merely as a means towards their own ends but as an end in herself, so too can Elina take that objective perspective on herself. The question is whether, when she does so, her dilemma "to be or not to be" receives the same answer as when she confronts it from a first-person standpoint. If not, then Elina's self-reflection has drifted on to the reef of antinomy.

But it is far from obvious that Elina, taking a third-person view of her life, is rationally constrained to judge it too valuable to be relinquished, even in spite of the soul-destroying tedium she daily endures. It is not always true that if something is a good then the more we have of it the better. Chocolate and Beethoven symphonies are both excellent things but it is possible to become satiated with them. Elina may reasonably conclude that her life has provided all that a good life should provide, not just to herself but to others too. She can fully acknowledge her status as an end in herself while disbelieving that her extinction would be tragic. Other people, she knows, are capable of taking her place, and filling it more zestfully. If human beings are not well equipped for immortality, then, *pace* Loptson, it cannot be bad that their lives end. It is misleading to say that death removes something precious from the world in cases where the subject has lived long enough to fulfil her potential and faces nothing but the "waste sad time" stretching before her. When a life has been a success, it is best that it should end while the going is still good. That human lives are precious does *not* entail that death will inevitably be an evil.

Elina's first-person distaste for further living is likely, then, to accord with her third-person judgement that she has come to the end of herself. One can imagine her, in her final moments, quoting from the Book of Ecclesiastes: "To every thing there is a season, and a time to every purpose under the heaven: A time to be born, and a time to die" (Ecclesiastes 3:1–2).

4 Facing death

The fear of death

In an article on death and the meaning of life, Kai Nielsen recounts a story about the Oxford philosopher J. L. Austin, who, when he was terminally ill with cancer, attended a talk on death given by the French existentialist philosopher Gabriel Marcel. Afterwards Austin is said to have remarked to the speaker, "Professor Marcel, we all know we have to die, but why do we have to sing songs about it?" (Nielsen 2000: 154).

What contrasts does this vignette point up? Oxford phlegm versus Parisian passion? Perhaps. The sober and reticent English approach to philosophy in the mid-twentieth century versus the more "engaged" philosophical style of the continent? Probably. Above all, the difference between regarding death as a ground of intense existential anxiety and seeing it as an unavoidable fact of life about which there is no point in making a fuss. Nielsen warns us against thinking that there was anything shallow about Austin's response to Marcel. The dying Austin did not take death to be trivial, nor, as we know from other sources, was he in denial about his own fatal illness. But he firmly believed that we do not make things better for ourselves by "singing songs" about our fate: a fate that no amount of breast-beating and lamentation will enable us to escape.

Austin's attitude may remind us of that of the Stoic philosopher and Roman emperor Marcus Aurelius: "Never, then, will a thinking man view death lightly, impatiently, or scornfully; he will wait for it as but one more of Nature's processes" (1964: 138). Death is an inevitable part of the natural cycle of living things; whatever is born must die. It is not just a matter of "what cannot be cured must be endured"; the Stoics thought that there was something singularly inappropriate about complaining about the way that nature goes about its business. On this view, it is not merely futile but improper to bemoan "the things that nature wills" (*ibid.*). Nature makes the rules, and there is nothing outside nature to provide an independent standard by which its operations can be judged. Why, then, get worked up about death and look on it as a thing of dread? In view of death's naturalness and inevitability, would we not do best, as Nielsen proposes, simply to "face it and get on with the living of our lives" (Nielsen 2000: 155)?

This may seem patently sensible advice. Facing death in a spirit of calm acceptance while we continue with our daily lives sounds a more constructive option than abandoning ourselves to existential anguish. Yet facing death squarely *and* with composure is not so very easy, especially as the end draws close. Neither the process of dying nor the non-existence that follows it is a pleasing prospect, however natural both may be. Nor is it obvious that we should look on death with equanimity just because it is part of the natural cycle. Why should *that* fact be of any comfort to us? Many things that happen in nature are antithetical to human interests. If nature is a mother, she is often a notably negligent one. The Stoic advice to align our personal perspective with that of nature can be challenged on the ground that even to attempt this would be to risk alienation from our own humanity. Nature, blind and unloving, "red in tooth and claw/ With ravine", as Alfred Lord Tennyson described her in *In Memoriam* (stanza 56), is hardly a good moral model for us. If it makes sense at all to ascribe a perspective to nature, it is far from clear that we should seek to identify with it.

The simplest tactic for achieving tranquillity in the face of death is to avoid thinking about it altogether. A more complex (if not always more subtle) mode of evasion is to pretend that death is something other than it is: a rest or refuge, a return to the womb of nature, a transition to a higher state, the culmination of life, a "graduation".[1] "Death is nothing at all / I have only slipped away into the next room" begins one well-know poetic exercise in death denial, which proceeds to ask: "What is death but a negligible accident?"[2] Too often, as McMahan complains, philosophers and "many otherwise sagacious people" have resorted to one or another "strategy of denial" (2002: 96).[3] The Stoic insistence that death, being natural, cannot be a bad thing might be construed as another example of such a strategy, although we should not deny the nobility of many recorded Stoic deaths, which were notably free from the kind of song-singing decried by Austin.[4]

But perhaps there would be some excuse for adopting a strategy of denial or evasion if death really were too frightful to look in the face. Confronted with a choice between denial or evasion of death, on the one hand, and "living" in a state of existential funk, on the other, we might find it preferable to plump for the former. Lord Shaftesbury remarks that the fear of death can oppress and distract us, and poison all enjoyment, even in "the safest stillest hour of retreat and quiet" (Cooper 1727: vol. 2, 143). While refusing to recognize that our "being-towards-death" would constitute a form of inauthenticity, this strategy, by releasing the springs of action, should at least save us from the equally inauthentic condition of becoming mere depressive navel-gazers. However, as we noted in Chapter 2, maintaining a proper consciousness of our mortality does not require us to be constantly thinking about death, still less meeting every new moment with the thought that it may be our last. Unless we are unfortunate enough to be of unusually neurotic temperament, we ought to be able temporarily to bracket off thoughts of death while we focus on the business of living. Such bracketing is not the same as thrusting those thoughts completely out of sight or self-deceptively attempting to mould them into some comelier shape, and it should enable us to retain an authentic attitude towards our mortality without succumbing to an enervating anxiety.

Although philosophers, like other people, commonly talk about "the fear of death", this phrase, as has sometimes been noted, is not without its problems. Jay Rosenberg points out that such attitudes as fear, dread and terror "are logically appropriate only to what could in principle be experienced, be lived through" (1983: 199).[5] If death – the condition of being dead – is non-existence, then it does not seem that it is a logically proper object of fear, or of any other attitude that we take to things we can experience. I can, of course, fear *dying*, if I have reason to expect that this will be painful or unpleasant (I can also fear *that* my dying will be painful or unpleasant, where I have no idea what it will be like). But it makes no sense to talk of fearing non-existence. It therefore seems that there is no need to look for subtle reasons why we should not fear death. The plain fact is that death – being dead – is not within the category of potentially fearful things.

But if I cannot strictly *fear* being non-existent, I can still look with great dislike on the prospect of my life ending, with the consequent loss of all opportunities for further goods (including the good of continued existence itself).[6] Even if I live to be a hundred, I am unlikely to have done all that I wished to do, and I may still consider myself "too young to die". When we speak about fearing death, we are talking loosely rather than talking nonsense: expressing our regret for the things of which death will deprive us. We might say that death is not bad "in itself" (that is, bad as a state of non-existence) but bad as a deprivation of opportunities. Other things being equal, we would prefer to live long lives rather than short ones, and youthful people can speak of their fear of dying young without being guilty of linguistic impropriety. As we shall see later when we examine the Epicurean claim that death, being a state of non-existence, cannot be an evil for us, the task of characterizing the misfortune of mortality calls for considerable philosophical finesse. It is surprisingly easy to fall into incoherence when we attempt to say what is bad about death. But we should not be in a hurry to abandon the firm intuition that death is bad for us because life is good. And if death is bad for us, and something that we hope will be long delayed in our own case, then it is not too misleading to speak of it as an object of fear.

Death will be more straightforwardly a fearful thing to people who believe that dying is followed by some form of afterlife that may or may not be pleasant. The sociologists Michael Leming and George Dickinson write that "[d]eath in the United States is viewed as fearful because Americans have been systematically taught to fear it. Horror movies portray death, ghosts, skeletons, goblins, bogeymen, and ghoulish morticians as things to be feared" (2002: 59). One hopes, for the sake of American self-respect, that this is a caricature, and that Americans do not acquire their basic ideas about death from Hollywood. However, Leming and Dickinson are right to assert that "concerns with the afterlife" are a major element in many people's fear of dying and death (*ibid.*: 61). In days when belief in hell-fire was much more widespread than it is now, the prospect of death was a truly terrifying one, as even the most God-fearing and upright folk could not be sure that there was not somewhere in their record some forgotten sin that would ensure their eternal damnation.[7]

Nowadays comparatively few people appear to have much personal fear of going to hell, and even many committed Christians are doubtful about the existence of hell-fire and tormenting devils. (Whether or not, as Sartre ironically proposed in his play *Huis Clos*, hell is other people, many contemporary believers appear to think that hell is only *for* other people, not for them.) But if hell has shed much of its terror for modern religious believers, the image of heaven remains as impalpable and indefinite as it always was. It is beyond our power to imagine what existence in the presence of God and the community of saints would be like, or how it could be satisfying for eternity. Consequently even those who confidently look forward to going to heaven may find their pleasure in the anticipation tempered by a fear of the unknown.

Alongside worries about the nature of the afterlife, we may have concerns for the people who have depended on us and whose welfare may be adversely affected by our passing. We may also fear that our physical remains will be treated with disrespect, or that our reputation will suffer damage when it is beyond our capacity to repair it. Since we will not be around to experience such things, it has been questioned whether they can constitute genuine harms to us, and so be legitimate objects of fear. We shall take up these issues later but should meanwhile note that fears about posthumous indignity, whether they are rational or not, are often intensely felt. It is reported that Hitler's mistress, Eva Braun, preferred to die by poison rather than a bullet because she did not want to be an ugly corpse. Many would understand and sympathise with her concern. And few people are indifferent to the reputation they will leave behind them or look calmly on the prospect of becoming targets of posthumous slander.

Fear of death, then, has many and varied facets. It is also seemingly unique to the human species. Although other animals instinctively flee, as we do, from life-threatening situations, and individuals of some higher species have been observed to manifest signs of distress at the deaths of family or group members, probably no subhuman animals have the conceptual capacity to envisage their own deaths. To do this requires not just self-awareness but also a measure of understanding of what death is and an inductive ability to infer from the deaths of others of one's kind to the fact that one too is mortal.[8] Further, as J. David Velleman and Fischer have pointed out, an animal lacks the ability to conceive of its life as a whole: to think of it as a narrative with an appropriate beginning, middle and end. Consequently it cannot fear, as a human being might, that it may be deprived of a good ending to its life-story: for example, that the projects it has pursued or the things that it cares about will be adversely affected by its passing (see Fischer 2005: 388).

While some aspects of the fear of death may be culturally created, it is intrinsically unlikely that all are.[9] For example, in some societies it is believed that any interference with the physical remains or grave goods of the dead will seriously disturb the soul's rest or hinder its journey to its eternal home. Such beliefs generate in culture-specific fears in the members of those societies about their posthumous fate. But it is scarcely necessary to seek a cultural underpinning of the universal fear of dying young or of the repugnance that everyone feels at the prospect of the end of one's world; these are much more reasonably ascribed to our natural concern for our own well-being.

Freud believed that the fear of death "reigns within us more often than we know" (1996: 152–3). Yet he also thought that we do all in our power to flee from the thought of our own demise; indeed, "our Unconscious does not believe in our own death; it conducts itself as if immortal" (*ibid.*: 152). Freud is one of many writers to have remarked on the difficulty we have in believing in the possibility of our own death, or of that of our loved ones. On an uncharitable interpretation, this failure to acknowledge that we shall die is another component of what Heidegger calls the strategy of "evasive concealment" (1962: 300) that we practise in the face of death.[10] But this judgement may be too harsh. Heidegger himself concedes that it is hard in the obfuscating world of "everydayness" to attain a genuine existential grasp of our own mortality (*ibid.*: 299–304). Another great German writer would have agreed with him. "Death", wrote Goethe in a private letter, "is something so strange that in spite of our experience of it we do not think it is possible for those we cherish; it always surprises us as something unbelievable and paradoxical".[11]

But how can we fear something in which we do not believe? Freud thought that the First World War would make it easier to believe that death was real and inescapable; when thousands were dying every day, death would "demand belief" (1996: 152). Yet one may wonder how Freud can assert that the fear of death "reigns within us more often than we know" if he thinks that we need such traumatic reminders before we take it seriously. We can relieve this apparent tension if we ascribe to Freud the plausible view that we *do* take the prospect of death seriously, thus supplying ourselves with grounds for anxiety, but only intermittently and reluctantly. Most of the time we are content to lose ourselves in "everydayness", but occasionally death forces itself on our attention, demanding belief. Most commonly this happens when people we love die, causing our world to take on an unfamiliar and hostile appearance. Even the death of a beloved pet can jolt us out of our groove of customary complacency. Gaita reports how in the presence of his old dog Gypsy he was saturated with the thought of their common mortality (2004: 72).

When people who are close to us die we often console ourselves by remembering the good things that happened to them or the happy times we shared with them. It would be wrong to think of this as merely an unsubtle means of distracting ourselves from the distressing fact of their death. A life that is over will typically leave us with much to celebrate and remember fondly. We can think about the dead without all the time having to think of them *as* dead. To do the latter would not only be to make ourselves needlessly miserable but would perversely divert our attention from the very features that made the dead valuable to themselves and to us. We are not denying death whenever we are not looking at ourselves or others as corpses-to-be and it is possible to be realistic about death without being morbid. We need not sit, like St Jerome in old pictures, with a grinning skull on our desks as a *memento mori*. To regard life as simply a prelude to death is foolishly to undervalue life.[12]

Courage in the face of death

It is a truism that courage should be attributed not to those who feel no fear in dangerous or frightening situations, but to those who feel fear and refuse to give way to it. People who are literally "fearless" (like the "hero" Siegfried in Wagner's *Ring* cycle) are blockheads, not brave. For Aristotle, courage was the virtuous mean between the vices of cowardice and rashness; and although we sometimes term "brave" people who act with a reckless unconcern for their own safety, courage, like other virtues, is at its most admirable when it is guided by practical reason (*phronesis*).[13] Risking our lives, our health or our goods without adequate reason, or where the odds are impossibly stacked against us, manifests folly rather than courage. The brave are prepared to take risks, but not needless ones.[14] The three hundred Spartans and their allies who held the pass at Thermopylae against the advancing Persian host expected to die but willingly gave their lives as the price of saving their country. Having weighed up which risks are worth taking, courageous people then display rationality in the presence of danger by keeping their wits when others are losing theirs. Instead of succumbing to panic or despair, they try to stay calm in the face of danger. Since courage, like every other virtue, comes in degrees, they may be more or less successful in this.

Often, though, we do not have the luxury of being able to decide whether to resist a threat or calculate what risks are worth running on account of it. There are many dangerous or distressing situations that we are forced to confront whether we wish to or not. Courage in these circumstances takes the particular form of fortitude: the quality of those who are strong (Latin *fortis*) in adversity. Fortitude is probably the most common form of bravery for people who live in relatively peaceful times and a secure environment. Those who are in this happy situation are less likely to be called to defend their country from its enemies than to be faced with the standard human ills of pain, sickness, loss of loved ones, betrayals and let-downs, emotional upsets and social disappointments – and, last but not least, their own death. It would be a mistake to think of fortitude as a merely passive virtue consisting, above all, in patient, uncomplaining endurance. Having the quality of fortitude involves more than showing to the world a stiff upper lip. It is the virtue of those who refuse to be ground down by their distressful condition and continue to pursue the things that matter to them. A person who is dying from cancer and who works right up to the end, as J. L. Austin did, provides a fine example of fortitude. This is a virtue of the strong-willed and active, combining resignation in regard to what cannot be changed with a determination to make the best of things.

Since death is one unpleasantness we cannot escape, it might seem obvious that we should meet it with fortitude. And this indeed is a very ancient assumption. Nevertheless it has occasionally been challenged. In Philip Larkin's poem *Aubade*, we meet the poet lying awake and thinking about death, the "dread of dying" and "the total emptiness for ever" that follows it. Since there is "nothing more terrible, nothing more true" than our extinction at death, nothing can dispel this "special way of being afraid":

> Courage is no good:
> It means not scaring others. Being brave
> Lets no one off the grave.
> Death is no different whined at than withstood.
>
> ("Aubade", in *Collected Poems*
> [London: Faber, 2003: 190–91])

These lines embody one whole truth and a number of half-truths. It is undeniable that we shall not escape death, however brave we are. But there is a lot more to courage than "not scaring others". "Cowards", as another famous poet wrote, "die many times before their deaths: The valiant never taste of death but once" (*Julius Caesar* II.ii.32–3). Courage is primarily about not giving into fear oneself, not about not frightening others. Nor is it clear that death is "no different", in any other than the crude physical sense that it will happen to us all the same, whether we whine about it or face it with spirit. Do we really help ourselves by "singing songs" about death? There are better and worse deaths just as there are better and worse lives. When death approaches, we should try to hold on to as much self-respect as we can.

But perhaps this reading is a little harsh on Larkin. The poem may instead be targeting the illusion that we can insulate ourselves from the reality of death by taking a high moral tone with it and ourselves, pretending that our virtue enables us to combat death and emerge the victor. On this interpretation, Larkin's message is that all bravery in the encounter with death is really bravado. No matter how much courage we display when dying, our virtue is utterly annihilated, as we are, by death. Why worry about going to pieces over death when death will reduce us to dust anyway? We may be as virtuous as we like before dying, but we shall still be as dead as Kipling's Danny Deever "in the mornin'".[15]

Yet while the virtue of fortitude cannot save us from death, it can save us from dying a worse death than we need to. The point of fortitude is not to defeat mortality but to maintain our status as self-determining agents for as long as we can. To give in to the fear of death and let ourselves be overwhelmed by the horror of it is to cease to live authentically. We are then effectively enchained by our own fear and lose all zest for life (ironically, since it is our fondness for life in the first place that spurs our fear of losing it). When Heidegger advises us to have the "courage for anxiety in the face of death", he does not mean that we should give ourselves over to whining. The thought is rather that once we admit that death is impending, we can direct our lives with a new freedom ("an impassioned freedom towards death") that is illusion-free (Heidegger 1962: 311). Such freedom is compatible with fortitude, and even requires it if we are to "put up with [death] as a possibility" (*ibid*.: 306) and resist the ever-present temptation to sink back into comforting evasion.

"Despise not death", said Marcus Aurelius; "smile, rather, at its coming; it is among the things that Nature wills" (1964: 138). But this Stoic advice is absurd; we may have to put up with death but we surely cannot be expected to *like* it. Facing death with fortitude may exclude moaning about it but cannot require us to smile. However, a more interesting question is whether fortitude is consistent with having bitter or angry feelings about death. At first sight, such attitudes may seem perverse unless we hold that some conscious agent (God, say, or a personified Nature) is responsible for the human condition. Yet some people who have no such belief have thought it unfitting or undignified to meet death in a spirit of calm acceptance. Those who regard it (in Loptson's words) as a "cosmic rotten trick" that we are capable of so much yet live for so brief a time sometimes take this line, even if they disbelieve in a cosmic trickster. Death, on their view, is *not* something we should simply endure with as much equanimity as we can muster. And if meeting death with fortitude excludes complaining about it, then fortitude in this context is no true virtue but just another form of evasion.

The poet Dylan Thomas has provided the anthem of this school:

> Do not go gentle into that good night,
> Old age should burn and rave at close of day;
> Rage, rage against the dying of the light.

Though wise men at their end know dark is right,
Because their words had forked no lightning they
Do not go gentle into that good night.

Good men, the last wave by, crying how bright
Their frail deeds might have danced in a green bay,
Rage, rage, against the dying of the light.
("Do Not Go Gentle into that Good Night",
in *Collected Poems* [1993: 148])

And so on in similar vein for a further three verses. The poem is a call to arms against death, represented as a blind and brutal destructive force. Instead of accepting death with resignation, as the Stoics advise, Thomas urges us to reject it with anger. This is not, of course, because he thinks that death can be overcome if only we meet it with sufficient spirit; there can be no successful rebellion against the fact of mortality. But we can and should protest against death's assault on our human dignity. Life may not always be beautiful, but death is grotesque. To accept death lying down, so to speak, is to collude with its wastage of us and argues a low self-evaluation. Thomas is in favour of singing songs. To remain mute while death destroys us is to fail to speak up for ourselves.

Significantly, Marcus Aurelius supported his assertion that we should smile at death by claiming that life is a cheap and tawdry thing, which anyone of good sense and fastidious taste would be glad to be rid of. "A man of fine feelings", he wrote, "would have taken leave of the world before sampling all its falsehood, double-dealing, luxury, and pride". Failing that, the next best thing is "to end your life forthwith" (1964: 138). A truly virtuous man, it seems, would commit suicide or, at the very least, court opportunities for dying. Once one convinces oneself that nothing in life is worth having, then one will have no desires that death can thwart.[16] No doubt a Roman emperor's lot at the end of the second century was not an especially happy one, yet the peculiarly bitter tone of Marcus Aurelius's observations suggests a man who has fallen radically out of love with life. One could hardly expect someone in this condition to "rage, rage, against the dying of the light". On Marcus Aurelius's depressive and depressing view of the "pestilence" of existence, the sooner we are dead, the better. But

Weltschmerz of this type should not be confused with noble resignation in the face of death.

This view that life is not worth getting worked up about is the primary target of Thomas's wrath. Gaita (2004: 97–8) has suggested that "Do not go gentle" might be considered a piece of fatuous romanticism, even the product of someone who was not very sensitive to the horror of death. It is hard to sustain such a reading of this life-affirming poem. Admittedly, to rage against the dying of the light may seem an over-theatrical mode of meeting death. But there are different kinds of song we may sing in the face of death. Singing a song of rage is not to be confused with weeping and wailing. Discounting poetic hyperbole, Thomas's injunction to "burn and rave at close of day" calls on us not to make a childish song and dance about dying (which would merely increase our own and others' distress) but to meet death in a firm spirit of *non*-acceptance. We must die, but we should die unwillingly and make our unwillingness apparent. It is true that a man of Austin's reticent temperament would probably have looked on even a quiet, dignified expression of rage against death as a song too far. Yet Thomas's alternative mode of meeting death with protest represents a serious existential attitude and does not deserve to be labelled as mere romanticism, fatuous or otherwise.

Is raging at the dying of the light superior to meeting death with fortitude? But these do not have to be alternatives. We can be strong in the face of death without being reconciled to dying. Having fortitude *would* be incompatible with throwing a despairing tantrum in our last hour but it is perfectly in accordance with the kind of grieving that Thomas thinks we owe to ourselves. The wise men whose words have "forked no lightning" and the good men whose deeds might have made more impact given more time, resent going so soon into a night that only the preachers of resignation can call "good" without irony. Thomas's rejection of all such dishonest evasion of the painful truth is as passionate as Heidegger's.

"To philosophize is to learn how to die"

Philosophy and death have often been thought to go together. In Plato's *Phaedo*, Socrates, shortly before drinking the hemlock, observes that "those who rightly love wisdom are practising for dying, and death to them is the least terrible thing in the world". Philosophy, he explains, depends on detaching the soul from the body so that, freed from its prison, it can focus on pursuing truth: for "it is impossible in company with the body to know anything purely", the body being a source of multiple "confusion and disturbance". Lovers of wisdom are therefore "everywhere at enmity with the body, and desire the soul to be alone by itself" (*Phaedo* 64a, 65a–67a; 1956b: 467–70).[17] Death should therefore be welcome to them, since by separating the soul from the body once and for all it opens the way to a glorious eternity of pure thought.

Socrates' philosophical enthusiasm for death obviously rests on some pretty large assumptions: not just that the soul will actually survive the body but that a disembodied soul will have the capacity to acquire knowledge without the use of any sense organs; also that philosophers are so single-minded that they will relish an eternity of doing nothing else but think. These assumptions are all open to challenge, although Socrates, as we saw in Chapter 1, does supply some rather feeble arguments in justification of the first. One also wonders how non-philosophers are supposed to occupy their time after death, if pure thought is not to their taste. The old adage that one man's meat is another man's poison comes to mind here. Unless the afterlife has some other satisfactions to offer, their eternity is likely to be very boring indeed.[18]

"To Philosophize is to Learn How to Die" (in Montaigne 1987: 89–108) is the title of an essay by the great French Renaissance man of letters and self-confessed melancholic Michel de Montaigne. Seeking to allay his own horror of death and of dying, Montaigne seeks inspiration in Cicero's suggestion that we should employ philosophy to help us prepare for death by tranquillizing the natural fear we have of it.[19] The way to do this, Montaigne thinks, is to look for philosophical arguments that justify taking a contemptuous attitude towards death. However, the costs of failing in this enterprise are high: if the fear of death cannot be dispelled, then "every other pleasure is snuffed out" (*ibid.*: 91). Montaigne is sure that happiness is impossible unless reason can show that death is a negligible evil.

Montaigne believes it quite hopeless to try to deal with our fear by paying death no attention. Not only is this a dishonest evasion but death is far too common in our experience to be ignored for very long. In the midst of life we are in death. People around us are dying every day and death has a disconcerting habit of turning up when we least expect it. (Montaigne provides a colourful list of examples of people whom death has taken by surprise, including a Duke of Brittany who was crushed to death in a crowd and the playwright Aeschylus, who is supposed to have been killed by the falling shell of a tortoise dropped by an eagle.) If we pretend that death does not exist, then its impact is all the greater when it does arrive for us or those we care about. Death-deniers are then in for a very rude shock: "what storms of passions overwhelm them, what cries, what fury, what despair!" (*ibid.*: 94–5).

A better strategy than ignoring death, Montaigne suggests, is to look for death everywhere. This way death is deprived of its strangeness and power to surprise. Therefore, "let us frequent it, let us get used to it; let us have nothing more often in mind than death. At every instant let us evoke it in our imagination under all its aspects" (*ibid.*: 96). In Heideggerian language, we should keep in mind that our mode of being is being-towards-death. Familiarity breeds contempt, so that by constantly thinking about death it should come to seem less terrible. The thought that death might strike us down at any time should also encourage us to make sure that we never put off until tomorrow what we should do today. Montaigne also seeks consolation in traditional arguments that death is not an evil. The final pages of the essay are a *pot-pourri* of well-known and dubiously consistent arguments drawn from a variety of classical authors: that it is senseless to bemoan our post-mortal non-existence any more than we do our prenatal non-existence; that once we are dead we shall not be in a position to regret lost life; that death, being nothingness, cannot be fearful; that death is nature's way of releasing us from the troubles of old age; that immortality would be tedious; that the important thing is not how long we live but how well we live (*ibid.*: 96–108).

Ironically, Montaigne's mode of "confronting" death seems in the end to be just another strategy of evasion. His spirited determination to keep death in mind at all times – to "stand firm and fight it" – sounds at first, as he claims, the very opposite of cowardly denial (*ibid.*: 96). The problem lies in the objective that sustains this stance: to learn to find death *contemptible*. "How absurd", he writes, "to anguish over our passing into freedom from all anguish" (*ibid.*: 102). We should certainly go gentle into a good night that promises relief from all the miseries of existence. Unfortunately this is just another example of the old ploy of painting life in the blackest possible colours in order to make death appear attractive by contrast; and it should only convince those for whom life truly is nasty, brutish and short. There is no reason to doubt Montaigne's sincerity when he claimed to be looking death straight in the eye, yet he was really seeing it through a distorting lens of philosophical arguments, some of them highly casuistical. While Montaigne was sufficiently honest and realistic to acknowledge the perennial temptation to deal with the fear of death by evasion, his own form of consolation for mortality fails to escape the danger against which he warns us. While it may be harsh to dismiss his observations on death, as Steven Luper does, as "a marvellous collection of inanities", it is hard, in the final analysis, to derive much solid comfort from them (Luper 1996: 108 n.3).

In one of the most penetrating essays ever penned on the subject of death, La Rochefoucauld fell into no such trap. Writing in the middle of the seventeenth century, La Rochefoucauld roundly condemned "that fallacy called a contempt of death" (1786: 27).[20] Although many men and women had faced death with great courage, the duke believed that no one, including any of the pagan philosophers, had been sincere in claiming to despise it. The very fact that philosophers had gone to so much trouble to prove that death was no evil showed clearly how hard they found it to convince themselves. In La Rochefoucauld's view, no person of good sense had ever truly believed that death was nothing: "for every one that views it in its proper light will find it sufficiently terrible" (*ibid.*: 29). We might wish that death were no evil but we cannot find good arguments for that conclusion. Reason, rather than inspiring a contempt of death, only serves to make clear its horrors (*ibid.*: 31).[21]

What, then, should we do if we find the idea of our mortality unbearable? La Rochefoucauld thought that there was only one thing that we could do. Contradicting Montaigne's advice that we should stand firm and fight our fear of death, the duke unblushingly recommended that we should "avert our ideas, and fix them on some other object" (*ibid.*: 31). What Montaigne saw as "brutish insensitivity", La Rochefoucauld judged to be an eminently prudent stratagem.

This injunction to look elsewhere if we find the thought of death too frightful may seem startling if we are persuaded that such evasion is dishonest. But La Rochefoucauld would undoubtedly have retorted that it is less dishonest than trying to fool ourselves by "vain reasonings" into thinking that death is nothing. In any case, he thought, we can always choose noble objects to distract us from the fear of death (as Cato and Brutus, for example, did) (*ibid.*: 30–31). La Rochefoucauld believed that the primary human driving-force was self-interest, and although this view has often been criticized for its cynicism, the duke's shrewd and surgical pricking of pretensions in his *Maxims and Moral Reflections* (from which the essay on death comes) provides an arguably more plausible view of human limits than is offered by philosophers of a more sanguine temperament. For La Rochefoucauld, we cannot live without a few illusions. (He would have agreed with T. S. Eliot that humankind cannot bear too much reality.) This did not, however, excuse philosophers who peddle the one impermissible illusion that we need no illusions. "The head is ever the dupe of the heart", thought the duke, although most philosophers were loath to admit it (*ibid.*: 63).[22] Since it was not within human nature to attain a genuine contempt for death, it was idle to counsel us to try. Philosophers should concentrate instead on helping us to find practicable strategies for coping with our fear of death. To philosophize is to learn to live.

Death and the virtues

Courage is just the most obvious of the moral virtues or excellences that we associate with death but there are others. Indeed, our understanding of what virtue is and the list of dispositions that we take to be virtues are heavily dependent on our sense of ourselves and others as vulnerable, mortal creatures. We might even say without too much exaggeration that virtue presupposes mortality.

In a famous passage in Plato's *Symposium*, Diotima, the wise woman of Mantinea, explains to Socrates that the primary spring of human creativity is the craving of the mortal for immortality. "I am persuaded that all men do things," she says, "and the better they are the more they do them, in the hope of the glorious fame of immortal virtue; for they desire the immortal" (*Symposium* 208d–e; Plato 1953: 540). All creative poets and artists, aware of their physical mortality, aspire to acquire an everlasting reputation through their works; but best of all is to attain a name for "wisdom and virtue in general", and especially for "that which is concerned with the ordering of states and families, and which is called temperance and justice" (*Symposium* 209a–b; Plato 1953: 540–41).

Diotima's claim, as Martha Nussbaum sums it up, that "the awareness of mortality stimulates a desire to beget value" (1989: 346) has considerable plausibility, although perhaps not quite for the reason that Diotima cites. It is unlikely that very many creative artists have been *mainly* stimulated by a desire to be famous after their deaths, although some have undoubtedly wished for this.[23] More immediate inspirations are the pleasure in the creative activity and the desire to be praised while one is still around to hear it. It would be even more unusual for a person to cultivate moral excellence mainly for the sake of laying the foundations of a posthumous reputation for virtue. That would be a very impure (what Kant would call a "heteronomous") motive for pursuing virtue. Virtue is normally thought to be something worth having for its own sake, as well as a source of further goods. Virtuous people not only enrich their own character by acquiring virtue but produce benefits for others when they practise it. Loving virtue and wanting to have a reputation for being virtuous are two quite different things.

If "the awareness of mortality stimulates a desire to beget value", the real reason is that our sense of our fragility implants a desire to live as well and as fully as possible in the time we have at our disposal. By wasting our time we waste ourselves, whereas by adding to the world's stock of goods we make an impact that we can take a pride in; we participate, with more or less effectiveness, in the kinds of creative process possible only for gods and human beings. There are many and various modes of creation that we can choose from. We may strive to develop our intellectual capacities or our artistic talents and bring into being works of art, literature and science. Or we can heed the advice of Diotima and join our efforts with those of others to create happiness in the family and justice in the state. We can also very appropriately, in the spirit of Dworkin's remark that we are our own works of art, pay attention to our self-development, seeking to eradicate our faults and improve our moral character.

The relevance and importance of virtue in our lives is also apparent from another angle. Mortal beings are needy beings, in ways that immortal ones are not. In arguing for the gods' indifference to us, the Epicurean poet Lucretius argued that such "immortal and blessed beings", if there were any, could have little in common with such frail and puny creatures as we are. Living in a state of untroubled peace in which nothing could ever go wrong for them, the gods would lack any stimulus to develop such traits as sympathy and pity, or value kindness, generosity or self-sacrifice (Lucretius 1951: 175–8, 219). If there are gods, they "pass their unruffled lives, their placid aeon, in calm and peace" (*ibid.*: 92), since it is "essential to the very nature of deity that it should enjoy immortal existence in utter tranquillity, aloof and detached from our affairs" (*ibid.*: 79). No god would ever need to feel sorry for another or seek sympathy for himself. Having no experience of pain, frustration, disappointment, grief or bereavement, Epicurean divinities would have scant understanding of what it means to exist, as we do, amid a sea of troubles. And because our experience would be opaque to them, we could not expect them to have any fellow-feeling with us, still less to come to our aid. Although Lucretius represents the gods as sublimely and selfishly indifferent to human affairs, it is difficult to see how they could be otherwise, given their incapacity to put themselves imaginatively into our shoes. As Adam Smith empha-sized (1976: pt I, §1), such imaginative identification is a plausible precondition for the formation of appropriate moral sentiments towards others.

Would such gods be better off than we are? Since we can only reply to this from our own perspective, there is a danger that our answer will be question-begging. Yet it is hard to distinguish the placidity of the Epicurean gods from mere lumpishness. The things that tend to be most precious to us are the things that we may lose. Would gods who could lose nothing care deeply about anything? Or would they simply take everything for granted, including one another? It is true that just as such beings would have difficulty in imagining what our existence is like, we find it hard to envisage what it would be like to live lives like theirs. Nevertheless, one thing that seems clear is that their lives would lack that ethical dimension which is a vein of gold running through our own.

One can conceive of gods of a less alien variety who are vulner-able to some misfortunes although not to the supreme misfortune of death. The deities of the traditional Greek pantheon were incapable of physical hurt but were subject, as we are, to such mentally disturbing states as anger, jealousy, envy and hurt pride. They had some opportunities for exercising virtue among themselves, but generally fewer and poorer ones than we do, since there is a limit to what can go amiss for immortal beings. For instance, it was never necessary for them to risk their lives to rescue other gods who were in mortal danger, or to give generous arms to save indigent gods from starvation. (However, one virtue that they might have required in greater measure than we do is the patience to put up with the tedium of an infinite existence.) Since there were bounds to the amount both of harm and of good that they could do to one another, they had less need than we have to develop their moral sensitivities or to be vigorous in virtue. Unsurprisingly, then, when we read the stories of the Greek gods, both their virtues and their vices strike us as mediocre by our standards.[24]

Human beings can be harmed in an almost limitless variety of ways. Even if we are lucky enough to get through life relatively unscathed by serious disaster, there is no escaping the ultimate harm of death. Paradoxically, though, our quite ungodlike vulnerability turns out to be the basis for the moral advantage that we have over the gods. Our precarious condition ensures that we have more and richer opportunities than they do to develop moral sensitivity and fellow-feeling. It is true that we also have more scope than the gods do to be seriously vicious to one another. But this only emphasizes the breadth of the moral landscape that confronts us. Writers on the theological problem of evil have argued that we need to exist in a challenging environment if we are to be capable of moral greatness.[25] Virtue and vulnerability are inextricably linked, and if our mortality is a cause of sorrow to us it is also a main source of our specialness as moral beings.

5 The evil of death

Epicurus's argument

In one of the most touching poems from A. E. Housman's cycle
A Shropshire Lad, a dead ploughboy poses plaintive questions to a
living friend:

> Is my team ploughing,
> That I was used to drive
> And hear the harness jingle
> When I was man alive?
>
> Is football playing
> Along the river shore,
> With lads to chase the leather,
> Now I stand up no more?
>
> Is my girl happy,
> That I thought hard to leave,
> And has she tired of weeping
> As she lies down at eve?
>
> <div align="right">(<i>A Shropshire Lad</i>, in <i>Collected Poems</i> [1939: 42–3])</div>

The friend's answers, given in the intervening and final verses,
are unlikely to bring the ploughboy much comfort. The living man
assures the dead that his presence is not much missed and that
things go on quite well without him (archly adding that it has fallen
to *him* to "cheer a dead man's sweetheart"). Intuitively, death seems

bad because the dead miss out on the good things of life. In the case of a youthful decedent like the ploughboy, the loss appears particularly severe because it is not just present satisfactions that are foregone but the opportunities for future ones that would have been available in a fuller lifespan. Housman's poem suggests that there can be subtler losses too: the dead ploughboy is gradually fading from his friends' thoughts and affections and can expect soon to be forgotten.

"Is my team ploughing?" represents death as if it were a point of view: the perspective of significant and irreparable loss, although the loss is not total since the ploughboy still has existence and consciousness. We might consider the dead young man's ability to communicate with the living as merely harmless poetic licence; yet the poem, for all the poignancy of its portrayal of premature death, encourages us in a false view of the dead as shadowy beings who have been ejected from life in the manner of unwelcome guests from a party. If the working assumption of this book that when we die we cease to be is correct, then there are no unhappy ghosts, of ploughboys or others, to whom we may extend our sympathies. (This may be just as well, since to exist as an impotent, frustrated ghost who sees the living having a much better time sounds a fate even less desirable than extinction.) We may still feel strongly inclined to conceive the evil of death in terms of loss: the dead, we might think, have lost everything they ever had. But this conception hits an immediate snag. The problem is that losses require subjects, yet after we are dead we no longer exist to be subjects of losses – or indeed of any other sort of evil (or good). If death is or involves loss, the loss must be of a very special sort, since it has the strange feature that it starts just when the subject to which it is ascribed finishes. All that remains of the ploughboy is corporeal matter, and we cannot ascribe the relevant losses to *that*. The ploughboy's body, which rapidly becomes one with the earth that he formerly turned, is not the ploughboy. Ashes to ashes, dust to dust – and, as George Pitcher (1984: 183) reminds us, dust can be neither injured nor wronged.

That the evil of death, lacking an appropriate subject, is illusory was famously argued by the Greek philosopher Epicurus, who set up his school in Athens in the first half of the third century BCE. His own statement of the case is short and succinct:

Become accustomed to the belief that death is nothing to us. For all good and evil consist in sensation, but death is deprivation of sensation ... So death, the most terrifying of ills, is nothing to us, since so long as we exist, death is not with us; but when death comes, then we do not exist. It does not then concern either the living or the dead, since for the former it is not, and the latter are no more.

("Letter to Menoeceus"; 1926: 85)

As many commentators have noted, two distinct strands of argument are conveyed in this brief extract. The first, contained in its second sentence, relies on another celebrated (or notorious) Epicurean teaching: namely, the hedonistic thesis that all good for human beings consists in pleasure and all evil in pain. If death is the deprivation of sensation, then it follows, thinks Epicurus, that it is neither good nor bad for us but indifferent. This argument, however, is open to the obvious objection that – quite apart from any difficulties we may have with its hedonistic assumptions – to pass from a state (life) in which we can enjoy the good to one (death) which can be nothing better than indifferent sounds in itself to be bad for us. While it is true that once we are dead we can suffer no *painful* experiences, the loss of all possibility of *pleasant* ones would seem to be a serious misfortune, particularly since Epicureans believe that if we manage our desires wisely and aim for the right things and avoid the wrong, our lives are likely to contain more pleasure than pain. But Epicurus probably saw this line of argument as merely a gloss on his more fundamental argument rather than as a wholly independent one. For he believed death to be deprivation of sensation precisely because he thought there was no longer a subject to *have* any sensations, painful or pleasant; and if there was no subject, there was nothing about which we could ask the question of whether it was better or worse off than it had been when alive. If, on the other hand, we were prepared to envisage as a possibility that the subject might remain in existence but permanently *unconscious* after death (a possibility that Epicurus appears not to have considered, perhaps thinking it too implausible) then the "no sensation" argument would provide independent, if not very persuasive, grounds for thinking that death would be "nothing" to it.[1]

What I have termed the "more fundamental" argument turns on the intuitively compelling thought that there cannot be a subject-related evil in the absence of a subject: to be harmed (or benefited), a person first has to *be*. Who, then, suffers the evil of death? Not the living, thinks Epicurus, for they are not yet dead; but not the dead either, as they are "no more". So death is never bad for anyone. QED.

Some philosophers have taken the view that Epicurus's conclusion is so patently unacceptable that his argument *must* be a sophistry. Thus for Steven Luper, "Epicurus's famous argument … is about as absurd as any I have seen" (Luper-Foy 1993: 270), since it arrives at a conclusion that no one – including Epicurus – could possibly have believed in, unless through self-deception. Yet the fact that an argument issues in a conclusion that is hard to accept seems insufficient to justify calling it absurd. If Epicurus's argument were truly "inane", as Luper claims, it would be hard to understand why it has attracted so much attention from analytical philosophers in recent years.[2] Not only have many contemporary writers taken it seriously but some have even professed themselves persuaded by it.[3] And although most continue to believe that the argument is a sophistry, there have been, as we shall see, several different diagnoses of what is wrong with it.

It might seem that the argument can be refuted quite easily by pointing out a false presumption that Epicurus makes about the nature of harm. For Epicurus, the only bad things are experienced harms (i.e. pains), just as the only good things are experienced goods (i.e. pleasures). However, it is plausible to suppose that there can be goods and evils that do not consist in positive or negative experiences and of which the subject may never even be aware. For instance, if Fred makes fun of Freda behind her back but Freda never finds out about it and no other bad consequences ensue, then something bad has still happened to Freda. Rejecting as shallow the view that that what you do not know cannot hurt you, Nagel notes that we would normally think it a considerable misfortune for people to be betrayed by their friends or ridiculed by those who treat them politely to their face, even if they never find out about it or suffer any overt harm as a result. True, if they *do* find out what has been going on, the distress they then suffer constitutes an additional misfortune. But they suffer the distress because they strongly disvalue what has happened, and not the other way about. As Nagel says, "the natural view is that the discovery of betrayal makes us unhappy because it is bad to be betrayed – not that betrayal is bad because its discovery makes us unhappy" (1979b: 4–5).

The bearing of this on the Epicurean argument is that if there can be misfortunes that involve no painful experiences, then death may be one of these. So while Epicurus is right to say that death is deprivation of experience, this fails to prove, as he thinks it does, that death is not an evil. For all that Epicurus has shown, death may be an evil akin to that of being slandered behind one's back and never being aware of it.

Unfortunately, this attempt at refutation misses the pivotal point of Epicurus's demonstration, which is not the unlikely proposition that all evil is evil experience, but the much more credible one that all evil requires an existent subject. When Fred ridicules Freda behind her back, the *living* Freda is the subject of the evil. Epicurus's "consolation for mortality" rests squarely on what Fred Feldman (1991: 205) has termed the "Existence Condition" that nothing either good or bad can happen to a subject s at time t unless s exists at t. (On this assumption, note, it would not be bad for Freda if Fred were to make fun of her posthumously.) Many philosophers have found the Existence Condition as cogent as Epicurus did. For example, Eric Partridge asserts that:

> the stark fact remains, uncompromised and unqualified: Nothing happens to the dead. … Accordingly, after death, with the removal of a subject of harms and a bearer of interests, it would seem that there can be neither "harm to" nor "interests of'" the decedent. (1981: 253)

Feldman's theory

Feldman himself proposes a different move against Epicurus. He suggests that Epicurus makes an illicit use of the Existence Condition, inveigling us into attempting a "life–death" comparison between the respective states of the living and dead, and then introducing the Existence Condition to convince us that there is really nothing to compare, since there is no way that anything can be good or bad for the dead. But we should refuse to attempt such "life–death" comparisons and restrict ourselves to "life–life" comparisons, thus effectively sidelining the condition. Feldman asks us to consider that an individual may exist at different possible worlds, at which he undergoes fates of different qualities, some better, some worse. To decide whether it would be better for a certain person, s, to die at a certain time t: "we must ask about the value for s of the possible world that would exist if s were to die at t; and we must compare that value to the value for s of the possible world that would exist if s were not to die at t" (Feldman 1991: 216).[4]

Readers should not allow themselves to be put off by the philosopher's term-of-art "possible world", which will be used frequently in this and later chapters. To speak of a possible world is simply to speak of a way that the world could possibly be. (So when Leibniz asserted that God had made this the best of all possible worlds, he meant that there was no other way God could have created it that would have been better.) Note that the actual world is one possible world, but that not all possible worlds are actual.

Suppose that in W1 (the actual world), our ploughboy dies in an agricultural accident aged sixteen. This world is worse for him, on Feldman's thinking, than an alternative possible world W2, in which he survives the accident to become a prosperous farmer and dies aged eighty. On the basis of this comparison we are entitled to say that the boy's early death is bad for him. This conclusion may appear to jar with the Existence Condition, but Feldman contends that the condition is strictly true only of what he calls "intrinsically bad" things (roughly, evils of which the person is a "recipient", and for which he obviously needs to exist), and that something can be "overall" (or "extrinsically") "bad" for a person beyond the temporal limits of his life (Feldman 1991: 219–20).[5] So the ploughboy's early death in W1 can be said to be "overall bad" for him because we can imagine a different possible world in which his life begins at the same date but ends later.

Feldman's account is initially appealing because it appears to capture the intuition that people who die young are deprived of the opportunities they would have had if they had lived longer. We reflect on the ploughboy's fate and think of how things might have been different. Of course, there is no guarantee that the ploughboy would have had a happy and fulfilling life had he survived the accident. We can imagine another world, W3, in which at seventeen he succumbs to a painful and debilitating illness and lives for another twenty years in misery. W1 may be overall worse for him than W2 but it is plausibly regarded as better for him than W3.[6] Still, given a choice between dying young and dying old, only the most pessimistic, who take a dim view of life's possibilities, would choose the former. Most of us would prefer to take our chance on finding happiness in a longer life. Had the ploughboy lived beyond sixteen, the probability is that he would have lived a life that was overall better for him. In the language of possible worlds, most of the alternative possible worlds that are "close" to W1 (i.e. are otherwise similar to W1 except that in them the ploughboy does not die aged sixteen) are superior to it from his point of view.

Yet despite its initial attractiveness, Feldman's proposal faces large difficulties. Properly considered, it really does little but repackage in the currently fashionable terminology of possible worlds the very intuitions whose coherence Epicurus contests. Instead of comparing the ploughboy's fate in W1 and W2, we could have compared his fate in W1 with the fate of his longer-lived friend in the same world. But until we have refuted Epicurus's argument, we are no more entitled to assert that the ploughboy's fate in W2 is better than his fate in W1 than we are to assert that his fate in W1 is worse than his friend's fate in that same world. The Epicurean argument applies to careers in other possible worlds as it does to careers at the actual world. Hence the need remains to supply some reason for judging that the ploughboy's fate in W2 is superior to his fate in W1, since in *either* world, so long as he is alive "death is not with him" while as soon as he dies "he is no more". The attempt to appraise the relative quality of his fates in these worlds must itself involve two "life–death" comparisons of the sort that Feldman deems illicit. It is only by thinking of death as somehow an "intrinsic" evil that we can judge that death in a *particular* world is bad for a person. But we cannot compare the quality of a person's fate in *different* worlds unless we can say how well things are going for him in *particular* worlds; otherwise there is no basis for appraisals of the "overall" quality of a fate-in-a-world. But Feldman himself admits that the Existence Condition, read as a principle about "intrinsic" harms and benefits, rules out the possibility of ascribing these to the dead.

Something like this objection, less technically framed, was raised by Epicurus's follower Lucretius against the view that death is bad on account of the good things of which it deprives us. In the third book of *On the Nature of the Universe*, Lucretius imagines the bystanders at a funeral reflecting on the things that the dead man would have enjoyed had he lived: the joyful home, the welcoming wife, the loving children, the worldly prosperity. Lucretius does not dispute that this is how things might have been: that, as we might say, it describes how things are in a neighbouring possible world. But he points out that as things actually stand no frustrated desires can be ascribed to the deceased man. Therefore, the mourning for his lost possibilities is misconceived (*On the Nature of the Universe*, book 3, lines 894–903; 1951: 123).[7] In part, Lucretius's argument is based on the contestable premise that in order to be deprived of something, one must possess a desire for it. But he is also pertinently objecting to the making of life–life comparisons across possible worlds in advance of a demonstration *that* death can be bad for the no-longer existent. In effect, Lucretius is accusing his opponents of begging the question in favour of their customary intuitions.

Feldman's anti-Epicurean strategy also encounters a second major problem. Even if possible-world comparisons could show that the ploughboy was comparatively disadvantaged by his early death, they could not by themselves demonstrate that his death at that age was an evil. Kai Draper notes that there are all sorts of things that would improve our lives enormously and yet that we do not consider it a misfortune to lack. No one would say, for instance, "I've suffered a terrible misfortune today, for I have not happened upon Aladdin's lamp" (Draper 1999: 389). Although it would be very nice indeed to find the lamp and be granted three wishes by a powerful genie, it is not a tragedy that we have not found it. So the fact that a possible world in which we find the lamp would be comparatively better – even very much better – than the actual world does not justify our lamenting our lampless condition. Reasoning by analogy, Draper infers that "the conclusion that death is comparatively bad is consistent with the Epicurean position that death is not, in any *troubling* sense, an evil" (*ibid.*).[8] More generally, Feldman-style transworld comparisons are intrinsically ineffective at showing which disadvantages are the ones that really matter, and why.

While both failing to find Aladdin's lamp and dying prematurely can be represented as comparatively disadvantaged conditions by drawing the relevant contrasts, they evoke, as Draper observes, quite different responses from us. No normal person desires to find the imaginary Aladdin's lamp but most normal people do desire to live long lives. Although this reflection does nothing to salvage Feldman's account, it may point towards the factor that is missing from it. If someone told us that his dearest wish was to discover the magic lamp, we would consider his desire so *outré* that, although we might sympathize with his shortage of wits, we would not feel sorry for his failure to find the lamp. As McMahan says, "pity is appropriate only in cases in which a person is unable to fulfill reasonable expectations given the circumstances of human life" (1993: 256).[9] Wishing to complete a normal life-cycle appears to be one such reasonable expectation, and that is why someone like the ploughboy, whose desire to live a full normal lifespan is thwarted, evokes our pity. (Note, though, that this approach cannot justify our feeling a collective self-pity for the brevity of human life. For we can no more realistically desire to live for five hundred or a thousand years than we can to find Aladdin's lamp or orbit Betelgeuse.) The trouble, however, is that when we pity youthful decedents we do so on the assumption that the desire for longer life we ascribe to them is rational. But if Epicurus and Lucretius are right, it is *not* rational, because death is not an evil. On their view, everyone who is alive is as well off as everyone else (being in equal possession of the gift of life) so long as he lives, after which he ceases to be a subject capable of suffering a loss. So why worry about the length of your years, given that your life will last as long as you have an interest in retaining it? Unless we can turn this argument, we cannot justify feeling sorry for the ploughboy. We seem, then, to be back to square one.[10]

Death and ante-mortem harm

Epicurus contends that death cannot be bad for a non-existent subject. So if death is an evil, we need to be able to identify a subject for whom it is an evil. A number of writers, following the lead given by Pitcher, have therefore argued that, in the absence of a post-mortem subject, death must be bad for the *living* person ante mortem. Even though death, as Epicurus says, is "not with" the living, the *harm* of death can be, on their view. We all have desires and interests that are liable to be frustrated by death, and the potential to attain a wide variety of valuable goods. Hence, according to Joel Feinberg, "[t]he subject of the harm in death is the living person antemortem, whose interests are squelched" (1984: 93).[11] He proposes that the harmed condition of the decedent began "at the moment he first acquired the interests that death defeats". Moreover, while almost everyone who dies has some interests that death defeats, death is most damaging to youthful decedents:

> [T]he person who will die at thirty is in a condition of greater harm on balance between the ages of one and thirty than the person who will die at eighty is between the ages of one and eighty. That is because death defeats fewer interests, and especially fewer important interests, of the latter than of the former. (*Ibid.*: 92–3)

It is not as odd as it may first seem to suppose that posthumous events can impact retrospectively on a subject's life. In fact this is just a special case of a more general phenomenon of retrospective signification. Whether Peter is now studying successfully or unsuccessfully for his logic examination depends on whether the script he produces at the end of his course will satisfy his examiners. Similarly, Paul's years of training to run at the Olympic Games turn out to have been vain when he is paralysed in a road accident on his way to the stadium. And an author is actually wasting, although he does not know it, the last years of his life if the sole copy of the great novel he is writing to ensure his literary immortality is destroyed the day after his death.

The view that death harms the ante-mortem person involves no metaphysically objectionable notion of backwards causation. The claim is not that what happens in the future can causally affect what has happened in the past, but that a person who was going to die young was harmed all along by his impending demise, unapparent though this may have been at the time. As Feinberg explains, "[t]he antemortem person was harmed in being the subject of interests that were going to be defeated whether he knew it or not". So if a man, Smith, dies young, "[i]t does not suddenly 'become true' that the antemortem Smith was harmed" (1984: 91) (although we might follow Pitcher [1984] in describing his death as *making it true* that he was harmed while alive). Instead, we realize for the first time that it was always true that many of Smith's ambitions, including that of living a normal lifespan, would come to nothing.

Even though the backwards shadow that Pitcher and Feinberg believe that death and posthumous events can cast on the ante-mortem person is not a form of backwards causation, some philosophers have still found it counterintuitive to suppose that what happens after death can have any bearing on the welfare of the ante-mortem subject. Thus Alan Fuchs asks: "Has Queen Victoria been harmed recently by the dissolution of the empire that she valued so much, and would she, on the other hand, have had a personally better life if Gandhi had never been born?" (1990–91: 346–7). In general, Velleman remarks, "[w]e think of a person's current well-being as a fact intrinsic to the present, not as a relation that he currently bears to his future". And we would not say "of a person who dies in harness, that he fares progressively worse towards the end, simply because he was acquiring more and more ambitions that would go unfulfilled" (1991: 339–40).

Although these objections by Fuchs and Velleman have some intuitive force, it may be less considerable than they think. Despite what Velleman says, there *would* be something peculiarly tragic about the death of a person who had recently taken up fresh projects or commenced new relationships to which she was deeply committed. Her death would acquire a special poignancy from the fact that the new directions her life had assumed had run so quickly and completely into the sand. And while Fuchs may be right that the subsequent decline and fall of the British Empire had no nega-tive impact on Queen Victoria's well-being, this may be true not for the subtle philosophical reason he suggests but for the simple his-torical one that Victoria's imperial ambitions were not sufficiently keen for those events to make much of a difference to her. Had she been, as the evidence indicates she was not, a fervent empire-builder in the mould of Cecil Rhodes or Joseph Chamberlain, then the rapid dissolution of that empire after her death *would* have cast a backward shadow of absurdity on her commitment to the imperial project. (Thus Rhodes's lifelong struggle to establish a British African empire stretching from the Cape to Cairo does seem imbued with absurdity in the light of later events.) Unless we take the implausible view that what you do not know cannot hurt you, we might consider that, on this scenario, the Queen's well-being would have been negatively affected by forthcoming events.

The claim that posthumous events can cast a backward light or shadow over a life that needs to be taken into account in any retrospective appraisal of it can, then, withstand the criticism of Fuchs and Velleman. Yet there remains some reason for thinking that the Pitcher–Feinberg line may not fully accommodate our intuitions about the harmfulness of death. To understand this, let us flesh out a little more the story of the ploughboy. Imagine that the boy was born in 1878 and died in 1894. One of his keenest long-term ambitions was to become a prosperous farmer with his own fields to plough. Pitcher and Feinberg would say that one of the many ways in which death harms him is by "squelching" this desire, and that this harm occurs in the period in which he entertains the doomed ambition. This is a special case of the general principle that all goods and evils that befall the ploughboy must do so within the sixteen-year span of his life. So while things may be good or bad for him in 1893, they cannot be similarly so in 1895, when he has ceased to exist. However, it is extremely tempting to think that the ploughboy is somehow harmed *after* death by missing out on all those things that he would, or could, have enjoyed in a longer lifetime. Whether it is taking a ride on the gleaming new traction engine exhibited at the agricultural show in 1895, or being the proprietor of rolling acres in the 1920s, it seems natural to date the ploughboy's misfortunes to the time when what might have been is not.

While the Pitcher–Feinberg theory plausibly identifies a form of harm caused by death, it is not clear that it provides an exhaustive account of the evil of death. The boy's entertainment of various never-to-be-fulfilled desires in 1894 would seem to be a separate evil from the non-fulfilment of those desires at their appropriate encashment date. The intuition that some harmful effects can be posthumously dated retains a stubborn presence, even in the face of the "no-subject" objection. Some philosophers contend that the intuition is simply misguided. For instance, Luper insists that we are harmed by *dying* (since this precludes our receiving any further goods) but have passed beyond harm once we are dead and non-existent. The problem, however, is that it sounds odd to say that the ploughboy is harmed by death in 1893, when he entertains a range of not-to-be-realized desires, but not in 1895, when he is actually dead.[12]

We shall see below (§ "Death and 'Cambridge change'") that there is a way of squaring our apparently conflicting intuitions about the timing of the harmfulness of death. It is possible to preserve the idea that there can be not only posthumously harmful events but posthumous harmfulness without falling foul of the "no-subject" objection to the notion of harm after death. But before we leave the theory of pre-posthumous harm it is worth glancing at a somewhat different objection that has been levelled against it. It has been argued that to claim that later events can make it true that a person was harmed or benefited at some earlier time implies a bizarrely fatalistic view of the world. According to William Grey, Pitcher and Feinberg get themselves into this undesirable position in the course of their efforts to rebut the suspicion that they are countenancing backwards causation. To this end, "Pitcher persuades himself, and apparently Feinberg, that posthumous misfortunes must somehow have been already antecedently attached to their subject", in effect being "written into the antemortem person's individual destiny". But this notion that our lives, with all their good and ill fortune, are already complete is, Grey complains, a "fantastic conception" (1999: 360–61).[13]

This objection is quite misconceived. The kind of fatalism involved here is of a harmless kind sometimes called "logical fatalism" and needs to be sharply distinguished from those "hard" versions of fatalism that claim that nothing that we do can change our destinies, since everything that happens does so in accordance with fate or kismet. The position taken by Pitcher or Feinberg is entirely consistent with the view that we play a role in determining what the future will be.

There is a famous discussion of logical fatalism in Book 9 of Aristotle's logical treatise *De Interpretatione*. Aristotle invites us to consider the truth status of the future-contingent proposition that there will be a sea battle tomorrow. Suppose, first, that this proposition is true. In that case, it appears that nothing that we now do can alter the fact that there will be a sea battle tomorrow. If, on the other hand, the proposition is false, then nothing that we can now do will bring about a sea battle then. So whether or not there will be a sea battle tomorrow seems, disconcertingly, to be wholly out of our hands.

Some philosophers have responded to this problem by denying that future-contingent propositions are either true or false. If it is presently neither true nor false that there will be a sea battle tomorrow, then the future can still go one way or the other, and we shall be able to influence the way it goes.[14] But there is no need to resort to the radical measure of denying that the principle of bivalence applies to future contingent propositions. (Note that it would not, in any case, be acceptable to Feinberg and Pitcher, since it would rule out the claim that it could be true during a person's lifetime that his interests would be adversely affected by his death, or by some posthumous event.) If it is true that there will be a sea battle tomorrow, this does not mean that no one *can* now prevent it, but only that no one and nothing is in fact *going* to prevent it. Human decision – and not fate, destiny or kismet – will determine whether or not there will be a sea battle tomorrow (along, perhaps, with other contingent factors such as the weather). If the relevant causes combine to produce a sea battle tomorrow, then it is harmlessly true now that the battle will take place then. In exactly the same way, a posthumous event can make it true that I am now successfully or unsuccessfully pursuing a certain project, where that success or failure is not already written into my destiny. If my project should fail, the fault will not be fate's but may well be mine: maybe I have not tried hard enough, or have adopted the wrong approach.

The symmetry argument

Philosophers concerned to explain the evil of death have often noted the striking phenomenon that while people normally regret the fact that they are going to die, they are quite indifferent to the fact that they were non-existent before their lives began. Is there some crucial difference between not existing before one's life and not existing after it that makes it rational for us to look with so much more distaste on the latter?

Epicureans were convinced that the asymmetry of our attitudes to prenatal and posthumous non-existence was irrational. In their view, if we do not worry about the first, then we can have no good reason to worry about the second. According to Lucretius, each period of non-existence is a perfect mirror of the other:

> Look back at the eternity that passed before we were born, and mark how utterly it counts to us as nothing. This is a mirror

that Nature holds up to us, in which we may see the time that
shall be after we are dead. Is there anything terrifying in the
sight – anything depressing – anything that is not more restful
than the soundest sleep?   (*On the Nature of the Universe*,
book 3, lines 972–5; 1951: 125)[15]

According to Lucretius, we should cease fearing death because
we have no better reason to worry about our posthumous non-
existence than we do to worry about the time before our lives began
when we did not exist. It might be objected to this that we also
have no *worse* reason, and that if there is an irrational asymmetry
in our attitudes it could equally well be removed, from a logical
point of view, by our coming to regret our prenatal non-existence.
Lucretius might reply that this would be psychologically impossible
for us, but he would be on firmer ground if he could demonstrate
(as he made no attempt to) the irrationality of such an attitude.
Probably he assumed that no one would dispute the irrationality of
regretting our prenatal non-existence. But relying on what people
generally think is problematic in an argument that seeks to establish
that something else that most people think: that posthumous non-
existence is regrettable – is wrong.[16]

Although some modern philosophers have defended the symmetry argument, most have looked for a reason to reject the counter-
intuitive claim that the attitudinal asymmetry at issue is irrational.[17]
Of those who believe the argument to be unsound, some think it
falls down for a reason first identified by Nagel in an influential discussion of the Lucretian claims. Nagel proposed that the argument
may be contestable on the ground that it is logically impossible that
a person could have been born (much) earlier than he is. While it is
logically possible that one could die later than one does, one could
not have been born ten years earlier, because someone born then
would necessarily have been a different individual. Therefore, if
one regretted one's prenatal non-existence one would be regretting a logical impossibility. And although Anthony Brueckner and
Fischer have argued that it is not obviously absurd to regret that a
proposition that is necessarily false is not true, there does seem to
be something perverse and futile about regretting something that
logically cannot be otherwise (Brueckner & Fisher 1993: 223).[18]

As Brueckner and Fischer also note, however, the actual time of one's birth hardly seems to be an essential property of a person (*ibid.*). It is generally accepted that it is essential to a person's identity that he or she was born of the combination of a particular egg with a particular sperm. It is also not very contentious that although one might have been born a bit earlier than one was if one's mother had given birth a few days or weeks sooner, one could not have been born (say) a decade earlier, because the same egg-and-sperm combination would not have existed then. (Even if one's parents had been born and come together ten years sooner, there is no defensible basis for identifying any eggs and sperm produced by them in that counterfactual situation with those produced in the actual one.) Yet it is not very hard to imagine circumstances in which someone could have been born much earlier than she was and yet been indisputably the same individual. Suppose that a human embryo is cryogenically preserved for a hundred years before being implanted in a surrogate mother who subsequently gives birth to a baby girl. This girl – call her Jane – could have been born a century earlier than she is. Would she have any reason to regret the years she had "lost"? She might, of course, wish that her birth had not been delayed if she believed that life was generally better in the century past. Or she might be pleased to be living in the brave new world rather than the dull old one. But, other things being equal, there would seem to be no reason for her to prefer one starting-point to the other, assuming that she could look forward to a similar lifespan from either point. The living-time she has lost by her late start is fully made up for by the living-time that she still has before her.

The case would be different if the time during which her embryo was frozen was time genuinely lost for living. It is harder to imagine how this might be, but we could suppose that while medical advances had made it possible to keep people who had been born a century earlier alive and in good health, both they and those recently born could expect to live for only another eighty years before some predicted catastrophe (say, a collision with a giant asteroid) would put an end to all human life. In this scenario, Jane might bitterly regret her prenatal non-existence. Had she been born a century earlier, she could, barring accidents, have lived for 180 years rather than a mere 80.

It is perhaps not inevitable that Jane would have this regret. She *would* do so if her primary interest was in having a longer rather than a shorter life. But she may also consider that had she been born a hundred years earlier she would by now have been a person very different from the person she is, and maybe one for whom she would have little liking or sympathy. Pressing a biological criterion of identity obscures the fact that our sense of who we are is much more dependent on our history than on our biology. This point has been well expressed in a critique of the Lucretian symmetry argument by Frederik Kaufman. Allowing that we can imagine circumstances in which the same person, in the biological sense, who is around in 1995 could have been around in 1895, Kaufman notes that the contents of the biography of a person who exists in 1995 will be very different from those of the biography of one who was alive a hundred years earlier. Although it is not quite so clear that what Kaufman calls the "psychological continuum" that constitutes the person in 1995 will be "completely different" from that which constitutes the person in 1895 (since it is reasonable to suppose that at least some aspects of one's character, talents, tastes and so on are influenced by our genetic make-up), the person who exists at the later date would find the person who would have existed earlier in most respects a complete stranger. As Kaufman concludes, "imaginatively moving a person 'back' disrupts the psychological self with which we are concerned" (1996: 309). And the degree of disruption would be much greater still if we imagined ourselves starting off not just a hundred but a thousand, or ten thousand, years sooner.[19]

It has been observed by Parfit (1984)[20] and others that human beings have a deep-seated bias towards the future, in that we tend to care considerably more about the good and bad things that are going to happen to us than about those that have already happened to us. It bothers us more, for instance, to reflect that we shall have to undergo a very painful experience tomorrow than to recall a similarly agonizing experience that we underwent yesterday. Some writers have regarded the future orientation of our self-concern as a primitive feature of human nature, Nagel, for instance, describing it as "a fact, perhaps, too deep for explanation" (1986: 229) (although it has been plausibly suggested that it may be a product of biological evolution). If they are right about the fundamentality of our bias towards the future, then it is not surprising that we find the Lucretian symmetry argument hard to swallow; we are simply not made to care so much about our *past* non-existence as our *future* non-existence.

From a philosophical point of view, though, it would be more satisfactory if we were able to justify our asymmetrical attitudes. And one significant difference between past and future springs to mind immediately: we can have a causal impact on the future but none at all on the past.[21] There may still be something I can do to avert or ameliorate the painful experience I anticipate having tomorrow, but there is nothing I can do to soften my pain of yesterday. Because we can influence for better or worse the way things can go but not the way they have gone, the future demands our practical attention in a way that the past does not. This does not mean, of course, that we waste our time whenever we think about what has gone. Not only do we draw useful lessons from our past experience but our concept of who we are is rooted in our knowledge of our origins; a being that had no thought of its own history but kept its gaze focused resolutely on present and future could have at best a very attenuated self-image. Nevertheless, the direction of agency is the direction of causality, and projects can only be pursued in a forward temporal direction. As self-interested beings, it is more important to us to think about where our next meal is to be found than about where our last one came from.[22] Furthermore, while we can have some influence over when we shall die, we have none whatsoever over when we were born. There are things we can do to delay the onset of our posthumous non-existence (e.g. adopting a healthy diet and lifestyle) but nothing we can do to bring an earlier end to our prenatal non-existence. Here is a very solid reason for being more concerned about our end than our beginning.

Still, even if I can stave off my death for a time, I cannot do so indefinitely, and that leaves the question of how it can be rational for me to care more that I shall not be alive two hundred years from now than I do that I was not alive two hundred years ago. My inability to identify with a person who would have lived two centuries ago may suffice to explain my absence of concern about not starting earlier. But my regret that I shall not be around two hundred years hence can be accounted for by the fact that, even though I cannot preserve my life so long, I *am* able to identify with a person, continuous with me now, who would be alive in two centuries' time. *His* interests I can recognize as *my* interests, since, although they might not be identical, they would grow out of those I currently have. However, as we noted in Chapter 3, the capacity to retain a unitary sense of self, as well as a reasonable amount of zest for living, may not be indefinitely extensible, and it is not the contention of the present chapter that death at *any* age must be bad for us. Indeed, the Epicurean claim that death is "nothing to us" would be just as false in the case of a person, like the aged Elina Makropulos, who lived too long as it is in that of a person, like the ploughboy, who lives too briefly. Death is "something" to both these decedents: an evil to the latter and a good to the former.

A satisfactory account of death's evil is necessarily pluralistic. Luper puts things in a nutshell: "Any reason to (want to) live is an excellent reason to want not to die; to avoid the latter, we must avoid the former" (Luper-Foy 2002). Most people have many reasons for wanting to live: a network of relationships, interests and commitments that tie them to life and that they are unwilling to relinquish. It is natural to become emotionally attached to persons and things, and to feel sorrow at the prospect of losing them. (Draper [1999: 409] remarks that sadness is an appropriate response to the thought of losing what one cares about even where the loss is inevitable.) Death causes us to leave our projects unfinished and our hopes unfulfilled, and it deprives us of the future as a space of opportunities for further development of our character and concerns. And this loss is connected with another that, as beings with a practical bias towards the future, we find peculiarly painful, namely, the loss of our capacity for action. Many philosophers have noted how ineligible most people would consider a life of pure passivity. Few of us would choose to be hooked up to a machine that, via electrodes implanted in our brain, feeds us a constant succession of pleasant experiences while we remain inactive and immobile. The problem with such a "life" is that we would be *doing* nothing in it. I do, therefore I am; our sense of ourselves as persons is intimately tied up with our notion of ourselves as agents. Stephen Hetherington has rightly identified our loss of ourselves as agents as one of the most significant deprivations we suffer by dying. At death we not only cease to have experiences but lose the ability to create the conditions of experience for ourselves. "Fundamentally", says Hetherington, "we are agents fearing the ending of that same fundamental aspect of ourselves – our agency" (2005: 414).

Of course, we could reduce the extent of the losses we suffer through death if we moderated our desires, pared down our projects, curtailed our relationships and generally did our best to avoid becoming emotionally committed to anyone or anything. But this would be akin to reducing the amount of potential damage that vandals could do to our property by first wrecking it ourselves. (This is the strategy Luper refers to as "thanatizing".[23]) One can evidently only lose a life worth living if one has a worthwhile life in the first place. Cutting oneself off from the things that make life valuable is not a reasonable way of blunting the sharpness of death. (Nor, incidentally, should it be confused with the detachment from worldly concerns recommended by Epicurus. On the Epicurean theory, we achieve tranquillity by pursuing the right kind of pleasant activities, among which philosophy ranks highly.) A stripped-down, fainéant life without emotional attachments and interests would be a life whose only meaning would consist, paradoxically, in its steering clear of anything that might give meaning to it.

If the Lucretian symmetry argument is ultimately unpersuasive, reflection on it nevertheless helps to reveal an important truth: that the evil of death needs to be conceived in terms of what the dead have *lost* and not just in terms of what they *lack*. We are equally non-existent before our lives and after them, but there the parallel ends. Before life begins we have lost nothing; after death we have lost everything. This general conclusion is only mildly threatened when we consider unusual cases such as Jane's. Although Jane could have begun her life a century sooner if her embryo had been implanted then, to talk of the time during which the embryo remained in a state of cryogenic suspension as time "lost" to Jane sounds strained. One undergoes a loss from a standpoint one occupies, not from a standpoint that one only might have taken. It is true that in a scenario in which Jane realizes that she could, for whatever contingent reasons, have lived a much longer life had she got off to an earlier start, she might regret the time that she has lost for living. But this problematically presupposes that she is able to accomplish the psychologically difficult feat of identifying herself with the person who would have been born earlier had her embryo not been frozen. Leaving aside such science-fiction cases, the conclusion stands that prenatal non-existence is inappropriately thought about in the language of "loss". To lose something one first has to acquire it. And to acquire something, one first has to be.

Death and Cambridge change

Suppose we ask the question: "*When* does the ploughboy suffer the harm of death?" We saw above (in § "Death and pre-posthumous harm") that it seems inadequate to locate the harmfulness wholly within the ploughboy's life, when he entertained a range of not-to-be-fulfilled desires. It seems intuitively plausible to say that the harm falls also in the years after his death, during the time that he might have lived. Had the boy not died of an accident in 1894 but lived a full human lifespan, he could well have survived until 1950 or later. While all human lives may be too short, the ploughboy's was particularly brief even by normal standards. So we might want to identify the first half of the twentieth century as the period during which he was most harmed by death. (In similar vein, Grey, writing of the early death of the philosopher Frank Ramsey, remarks: "The temporal location of the harm of Ramsey's untimely death, I suggest, is the time when Ramsey might otherwise have lived" [1999: 364].)[24]

But this response, natural though it may seem, immediately runs foul of the familiar "no-subject" objection. As Fuchs states the Existence Condition, "to be helped or harmed, one has to exist. There must be an existent self for self-interest, a living being for personal well-being" (1990–91: 349). It is precisely to overcome this objection that Pitcher, Feinberg and others argue that the harm of death occurs during life and afflicts the ante-mortem subject. We have seen that although this approach provides a reasonably convincing explanation of some of the evils associated with death, it has the snag that it represents the harm of death as being over as soon as we die.

Fortunately there is a way to preserve the "natural" thought about the dating of the harm of the ploughboy's death and also steer clear of the "no-subject" objection. To follow the argument, we first need to grasp a distinction between two kinds of change, namely "real" change and what is often referred to as "Cambridge" change. A change of any kind occurs at a point in time if and only if something begins (or ceases) to be the case then which previously had not (or had been) the case.[25] But whereas real changes are changes in the intrinsic properties that things possess, Cambridge changes are purely relational changes that happen to things in consequence of real changes in other things. For example, if John and Mary are married and John dies, John undergoes a real change – he ceases to be a living man – while Mary undergoes a Cambridge change from being a wife to being a widow. Although John's dying causes this transformation in Mary, the change in her is not a real one, in the sense of an alteration in her intrinsic properties, but a purely relational shift. Similarly, if Karen works hard to improve her chess skills and becomes a better player than Christine, whose skills remain static, then Christine undergoes the Cambridge change of becoming an inferior player to Karen in virtue of the latter's real change.

Next, note that Cambridge changes can happen to the dead.[26] Suppose that Tolstoy is presently the most popular Russian novelist but that at some future date he loses this distinction to Turgenev. It could then be said that Tolstoy had changed from being the most popular Russian novelist to being the second-most-popular Russian novelist. But this change clearly involves no alteration in the intrinsic properties of Tolstoy; it depends rather (as does the corresponding Cambridge change in Turgenev) on real changes in the habits of the reading public. Being dead, Tolstoy no longer *has* any intrinsic properties, since such properties can only be had by existent subjects.[27] But relational changes of the Cambridge variety require only that other things exist that undergo real change in relevant intrinsic properties. The moral is that a thing does not need to exist to undergo change, provided that those changes are of the Cambridge variety.

It remains to be established, however, that – contrary to the Existence Condition – anything good or bad can happen to subjects when they do not exist. Fuchs's claim that to be helped or harmed one has to exist may seem hard to deny. Yet reflection suggests it is false. During life, the authors Tolstoy and Turgenev were bitter rivals. It is safe to assume that Tolstoy would not have wanted Turgenev to surpass him in popularity *at any time*. If Tolstoy were to imagine this happening after both authors were dead, neither the Cambridge nature of the change nor its posthumous dating would make it any more palatable to him. For real changes are not the only ones that matter to us. People care not just about their intrinsic properties but about their relational (Cambridge) ones too. Marvin's pride at being the owner of the best car in his road is dashed when Mervyn next door buys a Ferrari. The fact that this is "only" a Cambridge change makes it no less painful to Marvin. Likewise, a poet such as Horace who craved literary immortality would have thought it a major evil to pass from fame to oblivion within a few years of his death. Cambridge changes and Cambridge properties can be the object of desires, hopes, fears and other intentional attitudes whose fulfilment or frustration is important to us. If Tolstoy becomes less popular than Turgenev, or if Horace and his verse are forgotten, then Cambridge changes occur to Tolstoy and Horace that neither man would have desired. Although neither will be around when the changes occur to feel disappointment at the turn of events, the non-fulfilment of their ante-mortem wishes and ambitions make those changes bad for them.

On this reasoning, things can happen after our deaths that are *good* for us, as well as bad. For instance, Horace's continuing literary fame is one such good for him, given his ante-mortem desire to be remembered. (Whether it is *sensible* for people to desire such things is, however, a separate question, which we shall tackle in Chapter 6.) This good pertains to him in spite of his having died. But in general death frustrates the fulfilment of our interests, since it prevents our pursuing the things that we value or enjoy; and even where our interests are posthumously fulfilled, that fulfilment will bring us no pleasure (although, equally, their *non*-fulfilment can bring us no pain).

But can *all* "squelchings" of the interests of decedents be characterized in terms of posthumous Cambridge changes? If not, then the explanation of the harm of death will remain significantly incomplete. For a clue to the way it might be completed, consider how we often reflect on what deceased people would presently be doing were they still alive. We say things like "If John hadn't died, he would be thirty this year/have married Mary/be a support to his aging parents/probably be a father/possibly be a millionaire". At relevant temporal points we record the things that would or could have happened to the dead person at or by that date, but that death has ruled out. Suppose that on 26 May 1898 the plough-boy would have reached his twentieth birthday. Therefore when that day arrives, he can be said to undergo the Cambridge change that from that point on it is true of him that he has *not* reached his twentieth birthday. Admittedly, this is a somewhat special kind of Cambridge change, as it is change in relation to the temporal frame rather than one in virtue of an alteration in some other thing's intrinsic properties. (To avoid confusion, we might wish to withhold the epithet "Cambridge" from a relational change of this kind, and regard it as being one of a sort akin to, but not identical with, Cambridge change.) Since it does not involve a change in the ploughboy's intrinsic properties, it is a change that he can undergo even though he is dead.[28] And its occurring is bad for him, in view of the interest he had in its not taking place (i.e. his interest in reaching his twentieth birthday).

Some of the other posthumous changes that affect the ploughboy are of a more straightforwardly Cambridge variety. Thus when the girl he leaves behind marries his best friend, it becomes true of him that the girl now has a husband who is not he. The event of the wedding involves a complex of changes in the intrinsic properties of other persons and things, in virtue of which the ploughboy is henceforth the suitor she did not marry (a prospect that would have saddened him ante mortem). (Note, though, that he does not alter his status of being the suitor she *would* have married had he lived.) Evidently not all the posthumous Cambridge changes that happen to the ploughboy can be so precisely dated. For instance, we cannot say exactly when the ploughboy is harmed by the fact that he has not had children, but if there were reason to think that he would have wished to have children in his thirties, then this harm can be approximately ascribed to the second decade of the century, when it becomes true of him that he has not had children in his thirties. In cases of this kind where the harm consists in things *not* happening that, had they occurred, would have been good for the decedent, the relational change might best be conceived as depending on the *non*-occurrence of relevant real changes (in this case, the changes that would have taken place if the ploughboy had lived to father children in his thirties). Those changes take place in a close possible world at which the ploughboy does not die young, but they are missing from the actual world.

Since all posthumous change is of the Cambridge variety, any account of how persons can be harmed post mortem (as distinct from ante mortem, as on Pitcher and Feinberg's theory) by posthumous events must have recourse to the notion of Cambridge change. Only this way can we sustain the intuition that death is bad for a person during the period that he or she might have lived. Ben Bradley remarks that "it seems preferable to have an account of the evil of death that makes its evilness similar to that of the evils of ordinary sicknesses and injuries, so long as such a theory can be made coherent" (2004: 4). The present theory satisfies this desideratum in so far as it represents the evil of death as "timeful" rather than timeless.

Some writers, including Nagel, might dispute the extent to which this is an advantage. They would prefer to say that it is *timelessly* bad for the ploughboy that he dies at a tender age, and would claim that we have certain intuitions that support this (1979b: 6). But it may not be necessary to choose between these alternatives. There is no compelling reason why we should not say *both* that the ploughboy's early death is timelessly bad for him *and* that he is especially harmed by death during the time that he would otherwise have lived. These judgements issue from different, but compatible, perspectives. The same duality of viewpoint is often adopted when we reflect on lifetime goods and evils. Suppose that James fails to gain the prestigious chair of philosophy on which he has long set his sights. We might reasonably think that the ensuing harm occurs during the period in which he would have held the chair had things gone according to plan. But we might alternatively consider James's academic failure shorn of any temporal index, as something that is timelessly bad for him, or bad for him *tout court*. These viewpoints are not in disagreement about *when* the harm is done to James, since only one of them is concerned with the temporal location of harm. In a similar way, we can say that the ploughboy's premature death is bad for him *tout court* and *also* that it is bad for him in the decades following his demise.

In this chapter we have looked at a number of responses to the Epicurean claim that death is "nothing to us" and, *a fortiori*, no fit object of fear or dislike. Epicurus's challenge, even if we ultimately reject it, as I have suggested we should, forces us to consider how death and events that happen after death can be bad for us. Nagel's observation (*ibid.*) that much that happens to us does not take place within the boundaries of our lives, while true, requires very careful articulation if it is not to strike on the rock of our non-existence as subjects after death. Some of that articulation we have endeavoured to supply in this chapter. But more needs to be said about the specific ways in which posthumous events and circumstances can impact on the dead. Many philosophers believe that people have interests of various kinds that survive their death (Feinberg has referred to these as their "moral estate" [1984: 86]), and that these interests can be positively or negatively affected by posthumous events. These claims need to be investigated in detail, and to this task we shall turn in Chapter 6.

Can the dead have interests?

> Nothing happens to the dead. No posthumous events can in
> any way alter a single instant of the full scope of events that
> constitute a completed life. Accordingly, after death, with the
> removal of a subject of harms and a bearer of interests, it would
> seem that there can be neither "harm to" nor "interests of" the
> decedent. Because in such a context, these phrases (i.e., "harm
> to" and "interests of") use prepositions with no objects, they
> are, strictly speaking, senseless.   (Partridge 1981: 253)

Partridge's stark rejection of posthumous interests rests on a simple
argument: interests require an interest-bearer; after death there is no
longer a subject to be a bearer of interests; therefore, there can be no
interests after death. And because there are no interest-holders after
death, neither, thinks Partridge, can the living have any responsibilities to the dead. To think that there are any such is to commit ourselves
to the absurd judgement: "We owe X to P, and there is no P" (*ibid.*).

In strong contrast to Partridge, Feinberg finds no conceptual
strain in the notion of a posthumous interest:

> I would like to suggest that we can think of some of a person's
> interests as surviving his death, just as some of the debts and
> claims of his estate do, and that in virtue of the defeat of those
> interests, either by death itself or by subsequent events, we can
> think of the person who was, as harmed.   (1984: 83)

Feinberg is quick to remark that he does not think of interests as entities detachable from their owners, as if each one were "a little person in its own right", capable of being harmed or benefited. Such a reification of interests, whether lifetime or posthumous, would be metaphysically far-fetched. Any interest must be *someone's* interest, and only people can be harmed or benefited, not their interests. The correct thing to say is that people can be harmed or benefited in respect of their interests. But it does not follow that an interest must end when its owner does. Feinberg claims that an interest can be said to survive its owner's death wherever it can still be fulfilled or blocked by posthumous events (*ibid.*). Imagine that an elderly man, Jack, is very concerned, for religious or sentimental reasons, that after his death his body should be interred in consecrated ground rather than cremated. If his remains are interred according to his wishes, then his interest in (what he sees as) the suitable disposal of his remains is fulfilled; otherwise it is blocked. Of course, if his executors act against his wishes, Jack will never get to know, or be distressed, about it. But as Feinberg and many other authors have pointed out, the reason why we are pleased when an interest of ours is fulfilled and displeased when it is not is precisely that we care about the objective fulfilment of our interests (*ibid.*: 85). Jack is concerned that his executors will obey his instructions regardless of the fact that he will not be around to witness what they do. The fulfilment of an interest is not to be confused with the satisfaction that its owner takes in its fulfilment. In general, interests can fare well or badly without our knowing whether they are doing so or not (unless they are specifically interests in our having or avoiding particular subjective states).

As we saw in Chapter 5, Feinberg's strategy for dealing with the "no-subject" objection to the claim that people can be harmed or benefited by posthumous events is to assign all such harms and benefits to the ante-mortem subject. So if Jack's preference for interment over cremation is ignored by his executors, on this view it is the *living* Jack who has been harmed in respect of an unfulfilled interest. If his executors were to take their cue from Partridge and hold that they could not owe anything to Jack when he no longer existed, the Feinbergian response would be to remind them that there *had been* a Jack, whose wishes it was their duty to honour. Alternatively, if we are uneasy about pulling forwards into his life all the harm of an event that takes place following Jack's death, we can opt for the more "natural" dating of the harm at the (posthumous) point in time when Jack undergoes the Cambridge change of becoming a person whose wishes have been flouted by his executors. Either way, to explain why what happens to Jack's remains sets back an interest, we refer to the desires he held in his lifetime.

This last observation may prompt us to make another distinction. Feinberg contends that an interest can survive its owner when it can be fulfilled or blocked by posthumously occurring events. But this conflates two ideas. There is a difference between saying that a person has an interest that survives her death and ascribing to her an interest during her lifetime in an object that will not end when she does (i.e. an interest whose fulfilment or blocking will be wholly or partly posthumous). In the first case, the interest itself is envisaged as outlasting its owner; in the second, only its object is. Suppose that Mary is keen that her paintings will continue to appeal to the *cognoscenti* after she has passed away. The issue is how Mary's lifetime desires relate to her interest in what happens in the longer term. If we wish to avoid any suspicion of reifying interests, then we do better to say not that Mary's interest in the enduring reputation of her paintings survives her, but that her ante-mortem interest can be fulfilled or set back after her death.

Such a view may be what Partridge (1981: 254) is gesturing towards when, following his rejection of Feinbergian posthumous interests, he proposes that the dead should be ascribed "quasi-interests" on the basis of the interests they have while living that certain things should be thus and so after they are dead. The introduction of a category of "quasi-interests" (the scare quotes are Partridge's), however, only serves to muddy the metaphysical waters. If Partridge's claim that the dead retain "quasi-interests" is motivated by a desire to avoid backdating to a subject's lifetime any harm or benefit that is posthumously done to her interests, then a resort to the notion of Cambridge change once more appears a preferable alternative. Just as people can undergo Cambridge change after their death, so too can their lifetime interests undergo posthumous alteration of a Cambridge kind. When Jack's executors ignore his wishes for the interment of his remains, his interest in being buried Cambridge changes into a blocked interest. Like the corresponding change that happens to Jack, this change does not require that its subject (the interest) should be currently existent.

By appealing to the notion of posthumous Cambridge changes to interests we can preserve the compelling intuition that people's interests can be affected posthumously without having to posit the continued existence of those interests after their owners' deaths. However, this line of thought will clearly not work in the case of any *new* interests the dead may develop, as T. M. Wilkinson (2002) has suggested they can in his essay on the ethics of research on the dead. Some people are perfectly happy for their bodies after death to be utilized for medical research. But others are not. Members of some cultural groups regard any interference with bodily remains or with their proper disposal after death as deeply disrespectful to the deceased, or even positively damaging to their soul or spirit. And many of us would feel dismayed if we thought that our bones would be treated in a cavalier fashion after we were gone (say, by being turned into fertilizer or fashioned into garden ornaments). Since none of these things can happen to the living, Wilkinson argues that the interests they infringe must be ones that begin when we die. So, for instance, "[t]he interest in not having one's remains desecrated is new, since one does not have remains while one is alive" (*ibid*.: 34–5).[1]

Yet we do not need to posit such metaphysically problematic new interests that arise only after death. Although living people necessarily do not have remains, they do often have desires concerning the posthumous fate of their bodies. It therefore makes sense to ascribe to them, while living, an interest in the treatment of their bodies after death. Necessarily, such interests cannot be fulfilled or blocked until after their subjects' passing; but this does not imply, as Wilkinson thinks, that they only spring into existence beyond that point. If Susan is concerned that her remains will be treated respectfully when she is dead, then, if that does not happen, we should say that an interest of Susan's has been set back posthumously, and regard that setback as a Cambridge change.

Not all the interests that people have regarding the posthumous future need be grounded on desires that they have in their lifetime. Nor do all desires relating to the posthumous future correspond to genuine interests. Having such desires is neither necessary nor sufficient for possessing the correlative interests. To see that it is unnecessary, imagine that people who believe there is no life after death are mistaken, and that the soul's successfully completing its journey to its eternal home is crucially dependent on the body's being buried rather than cremated. In that case, it is in their interest to be buried, even if they ignorantly prefer cremation. To see that it is not sufficient, suppose that Peter falsely believes that his soul will suffer everlasting torment unless certain magic words are pronounced over his corpse. Peter's intense desire that those words should be said corresponds to no genuine interest, since saying them makes no actual difference to the fate of his soul.

Can anything really affect us after death?

Peter's case gives rise to a disturbing reflection. If desires concerning the posthumous future do not automatically generate genuine interests that can be fulfilled or blocked after death, then it is at least conceivable that *all* such desires fail to generate genuine interests. Maybe when we think there can be such interests we are simply failing to grasp the finality of our own death. Because it is hard to comprehend from within the frame of our experience the ending of that frame, we readily slip into envisaging ourselves, once dead, as spectators of a world going on without us, where the places that we formerly occupied are filled by others. In Sartre's *Huis Clos* (*No Exit*), the dead journalist Garcin quite literally watches his living colleagues in the newspaper office as they prepare the next day's edition: "They've slung their coats on the backs of the chairs and rolled up their shirt-sleeves above the elbow. The air stinks of men and cigar-smoke. I used to like living amongst men in their shirt-sleeves" (Sartre 1982: 191). Although we may not take this scene seriously (any more than its author did) as an attempt to depict how things are for the dead, it is hard to avoid thinking of death as a perspective of some sort. As Sartre himself wrote in *Being and Nothingness*, "death is not *my* possibility of no longer realising a presence in the world but rather *an always possible nihilation of my possibles which is outside my possibilities*" (1966: 687). Strictly speaking, there is no way in which anything is *for* the dead. The dead are not absent from life in the way in which a child may be absent from school. The absent pupil is somewhere else but the dead are nowhere at all; unlike the child who has a possibility of "realizing a presence" in school, the dead have no possibility of realizing a presence in the world. But then how can anything that happens posthumously matter from a point of view that is non-existent?

We may take care to ascribe desires and interests concerning the posthumous future only to the *living*, who indisputably possess a point of view. But this is not enough to allay the fundamental worry. What requires explanation is how living people can *rationally* project reflexive concerns into a future in which they will not be around. The suspicion is that such concerns depend on the illusion that death is not really final, and that the dead remain in some sense subjects capable of being affected for good or ill. We may, in other words, be making a profound, if natural, mistake about the nature of our possibilities.

Partridge suggests that there may be another reason for our thinking (mistakenly, in his view) that we can be harmed or benefited after death. Taking as his example the concern that many people have to possess a good posthumous reputation, he concedes that from "a detached point of view" it is good for a person to be well regarded, even where he never learns of others' favourable opinion. But the trouble, thinks Partridge, lies in the use we make of this thought. If one were asked whether, given a choice, one would prefer posthumous fame or posthumous notoriety, one would undoubtedly plump for the former. He writes:

> But wait! Just what is going on here? In this very supposition we have utilized, simultaneously, two different points of view – that of the detached observer of good regard, and that of the subject of good regard. From the first perspective it is good, as such, to have a good reputation, even though unknown to the subject thereof. But then we neatly import this judgement into the subjective perspective and conclude that it is good for him to have a good reputation, even if he is completely ignorant thereof. It is by this route ... that one might be persuaded that unaffecting and posthumous harms are invasions upon a person's interests.   (1981: 257–8)

This is a puzzling argument. If it were true, if only from the "detached" (or objective) perspective, that posthumous fame was better for a person than posthumous notoriety, then he or she, while living, could rationally prefer the prospect of the former. And Partridge appears happy to countenance the reasonableness of a judgement made by a "detached observer" that it is bad for a person to have a bad reputation, even when she is unaware of it. But if it is *bad for a person*, even under the condition of unconsciousness, to have a bad reputation, then, tautologically, she is harmed in spite of her unawareness. Yet this conclusion is precisely what Partridge means to deny in respect of the dead. What he *should* be questioning is whether a judgement from a "detached" point of view that a dead person is harmed in respect of his posthumous notoriety can be true where that person is not only permanently unconscious of harm but non-existent. Given that the dead no longer exist to be conscious of what is said or thought about them, what justifies the living in viewing the prospect of posthumous notoriety with such distaste? Suppose that Judy, who enjoys a good reputation, fears that some enemy will plausibly malign her after her death, causing her reputation to plummet. This prospect – assume – causes her great uneasiness. If what she fears occurs, then what harm has really been done? For Judy's world came to an end when she died.

Many philosophers from Aristotle through to Nagel have thought of death as a porous moral boundary that allows for the possibility of posthumous goods and evils. But Nagel's (1979b: 6) claim that it is "arbitrary" to restrict the period of benefits and harms to the lifetime of the subject may seem itself to rest on little more than the contested assumption that such benefits and harms are possible.

Aristotle's intriguing if inconclusive discussion of the problem of the fortunes of the dead, occurs in the first book of the *Nicomachean Ethics*. Aristotle begins by citing the assumption, which was evidently as current in his day as in ours, that "good and evil … exist for a dead man, as much as for one who is alive but not aware of them; e.g. honours and dishonours and all the good or bad fortunes of children, and in general of descendants" (1100a; 1954: 19). To suppose that the fate of a man's friends should not affect his happiness, even when he is dead, Aristotle calls "a very unfriendly doctrine, and one opposed to the opinions men hold" (1101a; 1954: 22). Yet he resists the idea that what happens after death can make a critical difference to whether a person is *eudaimon* (happy or flourishing). To think otherwise is implicitly to allow that even the best of lives can be spoiled by things that happen after death – a view that Aristotle is reluctant to accept because it threatens his theory of the good life as consisting above all in the development and exercise of the moral and intellectual virtues (*aretai*). Since possession of the virtues is the most significant factor in determining whether a person is *eudaimon*, there are limits to the degree to which virtuous lives can be damaged (or, for that matter, improved) by external events, either ante mortem or posthumous. Even someone like King Priam of Troy, for whom things went disastrously wrong in his last years, did not have his life ruined so long as he retained his virtue (although such bad fortune may have prevented him from becoming *makarios*, or supremely happy) (1101a; 1954: 21). In short, thinks Aristotle:

> it seems, from these considerations, that even if anything whether good or evil, penetrates to [the dead], it must be something weak and negligible, either in itself or for them, or if not, at least it must be such in degree and kind as not to make happy those who are not happy nor to take away their blessedness from those who are.   (1101b; 1954: 23)

The reference in this passage to things "penetrating" to the dead suggests that Aristotle takes the deceased to retain some form of conscious existence and at least a residual capacity to be pleased or pained. Unfortunately, neither here nor in other works does he enlarge on the notion of posthumous consciousness. Since its consistency with the psychological theory he develops elsewhere is dubious at best, it may be that its cameo appearance in the *Nicomachean Ethics* is simply a complaisant concession to popular belief in a work whose topic is ethics rather than psychology. However this may be, Aristotle's vagueness over how the dead can be harmed or benefited is tantalising and unsatisfactory.

In an interesting recent essay, Dominic Scott has suggested that hints towards a more interesting theory of posthumous fortune can be glimpsed in the pages of the *Nicomachean Ethics*. On Scott's reading, Aristotle anticipates the view of Pitcher: that events occurring after her death can be retrospectively significant for a person's life. Thus if someone devotes considerable time and effort to bringing up children who will lead good and successful lives, then

their subsequent good behaviour and achievements will, in Scott's words, "make it true that the life of the ante-mortem person was a success in productive terms" (2000: 226). Virtuous people can be expected to engage in two kinds of activity, labelled by Aristotle *praxis* and *poiēsis*. In instances of *praxis* the goal of the activity is internal and the activity provides its own sufficient justification: for example, a generous person performs generous acts because generous acts are intrinsically worth performing, being fine and noble in themselves. But virtuous people will also engage in *poiēsis*, or productive activity, where the object is to promote certain external goals. (Note that the two kinds of activity sometimes merge, as when a person gives money for the sake of being generous *and* to save a starving child.) When we act with an external end in view, our activity can be complete only when that end is attained; and in the case of some productive activities (e.g. raising children to be happy after one's own death) that attainment will be posthumous. Aristotle is at pains to emphasize the importance of our productive activity to our sense of self; typically we identify ourselves with our projects and love the products of our *poiēsis*. In Book 9 he remarks that "we exist by virtue of activity (i.e. by living and acting), and ... the handiwork *is*, in a sense, the producer in activity" (*Nicomachean Ethics* 1168a: 1954: 233). Implicitly, then, posthumous events not only have an important bearing on whether a person's life has been productively successful (although they make no difference to the goods obtained through *praxis*): they also provide a form of survival of death, in so far as a producer can be identified with her handiwork.[2]

This account may better be described as one that Aristotle waves towards rather than one that he articulates explicitly. It also faces one major problem of consistency. If, as Aristotle repeatedly urges, the crucial requirement for *eudaimonia* is to realize in adequate measure the internal goods of virtuous activity, then it is hard to see how posthumous events, which cannot increase or decrease those goods, can make more than a marginal impact on a person's well-being. This account of *eudaimonia* sits uneasily with the idea adumbrated in Book 9 that our self-realization consists at least in part in the successful production of the external goods we aim at: the idea needed to sustain the claim that posthumous fulfilments and failures of our projects have a major bearing on our well-being.

Aristotle's view that it is natural to care about the fortunes of our children and friends after we are dead reminds us that there are other grounds than self-interest for being concerned about the posthumous future. If we care that our children will flourish after we are gone, we are unlikely to want this merely because their success will be good for us, fulfilling one of our projects. Making the best possible provision for our children to lead flourishing lives is unlikely to *be* one of our projects unless we sincerely care about our children's well-being. (Other motivations – such as wanting to produce descendants whose careers will reflect glory on us – are imaginable but less likely.) Because we love our children, we want the best for them; and we want this for *their* sake rather than our own.

There can thus be non-self-interested reasons for caring about the posthumous future even if it should be true that nothing that happens after death can affect our own interests. For if our world comes to an end when we die, other people's worlds will not. Since we know that people we care about will be around when we are not, there is nothing unreasonable about engaging in productive activity designed to advance their interests after we are gone. Indeed, if we truly care about them, it would be unreasonable *not* to do what we can for them while we still have the means. Doing nothing may also be unethical, where we have relevant responsibilities towards dependants.

But what should we conclude about *our own* interests after death? Aristotle's account of *poiēsis* supports the idea, defended by Pitcher and Feinberg, that posthumous events can be retrospectively significant for the success or failure of our lifetime projects. If this is right, then there can be rational grounds for self-interested concern with aspects of the posthumous future. Such concern is ultimately a form of concern about our fortunes *before* death and, as such, sidesteps any difficulties of the "missing subject" type. However, we should be cautious about assuming that lifetime projects that can be fulfilled or blocked by posthumous events are rational just because they escape objection on this score. If there needs to be a self for self-interest, there also needs to be a genuine interest.

Suppose that I am deeply committed to laying the foundation of my posthumous fame by composing deathless verse. If I succeed in this ambition, then my poetry-writing has been fruitful; if not, it has been fruitless. Either way, Pitcher and Feinberg would hold that the

profit or loss of the enterprise accrues to me during my lifetime. But if people read my verse for centuries to come, what good can that really do me while alive? I cannot take any satisfaction during my lifetime in something that I do not know will be a fact, while after my death I will be utterly oblivious to whether people are reading my work or not. Of course, I may have written my verse with the chief intention of bringing a little sunshine into others' dull lives. This benevolent, if vain, ambition is at least intelligibly focused on producing a benefit for conscious subjects. The problem is to make sense of my project under its reflexive aspect: to understand how its fulfilment can be good for me. We have seen that people can be harmed or benefited by things of which they are unaware. So my unawareness, while living, that my verse will achieve the undying fame I hope for does not rule out that outcome's benefiting me ante mortem, via the fact that I really am writing deathless verse. Yet it is hard to dispel a sense that there is something perverse about my dedication to the pursuit of a goal of whose attainment I can never be aware. Would I – could I – retain my ambition for posthumous celebrity if I had fully grasped the absoluteness of my extinction at death? Have I truly understood that death is "the nihilation of my possibles which is outside my possibilities"?

Rational or not, such self-concern centred on the posthumous future comes so instinctively to us that it would be hard, if not impossible, to abandon it. In part this may be owing to the robustness of the illusion that we retain a point of view after death. It may also reflect the ingrained bias of our interests towards the future noted by Parfit, Nagel and others. As we saw in Chapter 5, our disposition to care much more about the good and evil awaiting us in the future than about that experienced in the past appears to be a fundamental and inescapable feature of our psychology. From a practical perspective, the bias has an obvious survival advantage, since we can influence the course of future events but not past ones. Once we are dead, of course, the issue of our survival no longer arises. But our self-concern may be hard to "switch off", even when it is the posthumous future we are contemplating. The strength of our bias towards the future may reinforce the fantasy that our interests will go on and on, even beyond death. Yet the fact, if it is one, that we are naturally constructed to believe that posthumous events can be good or bad for us does not suffice to show that belief to be true. The stubborn difficulty remains the non-existence after death of a person to be the subject of goods or ills.

Posthumous events and the meaning of life

There is one avenue we have not yet explored. Earlier, when considering Partridge's distinction between the subjective and the "detached" perspectives that may be taken on a person and her life, we questioned whether a judgement from the "detached" (or objective) perspective that a dead person was harmed in respect of being posthumously notorious could be true when that person no longer existed. How could it matter to someone to be maligned after her death if she and her world had come to an end? Even a judgement made from the "detached" perspective has to relate to a real subject. But there may be an escape route from this difficulty.

One of the things we care about deeply is that our lives will appear meaningful when seen from an objective point of view. We find it hard to reap much satisfaction from our activities, projects and achievements unless we believe that they measure up well by external standards. Besides desiring that particular things we do should be worthwhile we are also concerned that our lives as a whole should be so. Nagel speaks of us wanting to matter to ourselves "from the outside" (1987: 101). And David Cooper has described human beings as "inveterately teleological beings" who actively seek for "meanings that lend sense and point to their activities" (2003: 126). The world we create for ourselves is a world of ends and purposes and we typically seek a rationale for particular things we do by reference to more encompassing purposes. When we ask why we should do X or Y – or why we should live at all – we want to know how X or Y – or life itself – are embedded in larger structures.

The fundamental interest we have in living a meaningful human life gives rise to various subordinate interests, some of which have posthumous scope. We have interests that stretch beyond death because what happens posthumously can bear on the significance that our lives and their component activities and enterprises have within a broader frame. If I pen what I hope is immortal verse, I know that I shall not be around to enjoy the posthumous applause it brings me (if any). But I can still aspire to provide a measure of justification for my existence by making a contribution to a larger

human life than my own. My objective, although not guaranteed of success, is that my life shall have value, from a detached point of view, within a greater scheme of things.

Retaining a place in the minds of others after one's death is some evidence that one has made an impact on the broader scene, and that the significance of one's life transcends its own limit. Being remembered by posterity means that our lives are resonating beyond their temporal close. Some individuals continue in death to shape the experience of the living more profoundly than many who are still alive (think of Shakespeare or Beethoven), but even lesser mortals can leave some mark on the consciousness of their successors. This thought can bring comfort when we reflect on the absoluteness of our personal extinction.

In the seventeenth century, Sir Thomas Browne summed up the common fear of being forgotten in some sonorous words: "For Oblivion is a kind of Annihilation, and for things to be as though they had not been is like unto never being" (Browne 1969: 242). Robert Nozick makes a similar point in plainer language: "People do seem to think it important to continue to be around somehow. The root notion seems to be this one: it shouldn't *ever* be as if you had never existed at all." If one's life makes no lasting difference to anyone or anything, one might just as well not have been born: "A significant life leaves its mark on the world" (1981: 582).[3]

These positions are perhaps overstated. It is not clear that significant lives must make an impact posthumously. If that were so, then the lives of the last people on earth would be doomed to absurdity. A person could make an important contribution to the human good during her lifetime yet leave little impact on the lives of those who follow her. To judge that her life was therefore insignificant would be harsh and ungenerous. It is better to hold that making a posthumous impact is *one* way in which a life may acquire meaning, but not necessarily the only one.

Furthermore, not just any kind of lasting mark renders a life significant. Some people are posthumously famous for bad or unworthy things. Consider this surprising case from Valerius Maximus's essay "On the Love of Glory":

> There was a certain man who determined to burn down the temple of Diana at Ephesus, in order that the destruction of

so magnificent a work should spread his fame throughout the world. He confessed this insane intention when on the rack. The Ephesians wisely decided to abolish by decree the memory of so wicked a man; but the eloquent Theopompus has named him in his histories. (1998: book VIII.14.15, my translation)[4]

The arsonist must have known the penalties that his crime would incur yet he willingly accepted torture and death as the price of a fame that could only be posthumous. Since his name (Herostratos) is still remembered over two millennia later, his incendiary scheme was on its own terms a great success. Yet it is hard to see the burning down of one of the greatest buildings of antiquity as an entirely sane act. To commit a capital offence with the object of keeping one's memory green argues, to say the least, an unusual valuation of utilities. Someone's life would have to be peculiarly bleak or his self-esteem particularly low for this even to begin to seem a good bargain.

Like some later perpetrators of eye-catching atrocities, Herostratos was probably an individual of low self-worth who believed that the memorableness of his deed would make his meaningless life meaningful. From being Herostratos the nobody he would henceforth be Herostratos the famous incendiary. But he may have confused an act that distinguishes a person from others with one that imparts distinction to the agent. His bid for fame showed contempt for moral and aesthetic values and left the world a worse place. Lacking an ambition to accomplish anything worthwhile, he wished to achieve significance simply by doing something memorable. But what is remembered about Herostratos is precisely the pointless stupidity of the man and his project. If his was a strategy for evading absurdity, it was self-defeating in its own absurdity. Leaving a mark like this on the world does not render a life significant.

Our concern with the meaning of what we do lies at the heart of our practical rationality. To "act" without point seems scarcely to act at all but merely to make bodily movements. The *Nicomachean Ethics* famously opens with Aristotle's observation that "Every art and every inquiry, and similarly every action and pursuit, is thought to aim at some good" (1094a; 1954: 1). Most questions about meaning are questions about the point or purpose of our activities and interests, and they are mostly answered by specifying the further end or ends that they subserve. (In the case of activities with internal ends, the internal ends themselves call for justification. We may play the flute for the sake of playing the flute, but why is this a worthwhile activity?) But this mode of justification raises an obvious problem. Suppose we say that the point of doing A is that it subserves B, and that the point of doing B is that it subserves C, and so on.[5] Where should this account stop? If everything we chose were chosen for the sake of something else, then, as Aristotle remarks, "the process would go on to infinity, so that our desire would be empty and vain" (1094a; 1954: 2). Later terms in the sequence supply the justification for earlier ones, but if there is no last term to be posited, then nothing seems to be justified. What is needed to stop the regress is something whose point requires no further justification: something that supplies its own sufficient purpose.

It is easy to see how such reflections can prompt us to "go cosmic" and look for the ultimate guarantor of the meaning of human life in something outside ourselves. Any answer that restricts itself to the human realm – such as Aristotle's that the proper purpose of human life is to achieve a happy or flourishing life distinguished by excellences of mind and character – seems to invite the challenge: "Yes, but what is human life *for*? Why does it matter that beings like us should live flourishing lives (or any lives at all)?"

Actually, even "going cosmic" may not suffice to stop the regress. Suppose that the living of flourishing human lives really was a significant feature of the universe. (It may be, for instance, that ours is the most complex form of life that will ever exist.) Yet even if human beings were the brightest jewels in the universal crown, the question could still be posed of what the cosmos itself was for. Might the Big Bang have been just a loud noise? Whether or not big is beautiful, it is not necessarily meaningful. Maybe the real tragedy of the universe is that so much exists to so little purpose.

Some people, such as Tolstoy, have thought that the regress can be brought to a close in God. But it is no clearer that we can non-question-beggingly represent God as the source of all meaning (the prime meaning) than we can non-question-beggingly represent him as the first cause or prime mover. The question "What is the point of God?", although shocking to many ears, is not obviously absurd. As Nagel writes, "Can there really be something which gives point to everything else by encompassing it, but which couldn't have, or need, any point itself?" The difficulty here is to see how there could be something "whose point can't be questioned from outside because there is no outside" (1987: 100).

Should we therefore conclude that nothing ultimately really matters? We do not have to. A more attractive alternative is to jump off the rollercoaster of regress before it exits the human realm. We want to feel that our lives have significance within some larger scheme of things but there is no reason why that scheme should be as large as the universe. To say this is to concede that humanity and its concerns may have no importance whatsoever from the cosmic point of view. But why should that worry us, given that our own perspective is not that of the universe? Shakespeare's plays may be valueless *sub specie aeternitatis*. Yet to conclude from this that Shakespeare's achievement has been vastly overrated would be silly. Tolstoy thought that nothing about human life, no matter how admirable when judged from a purely human perspective, can have any genuine cosmic significance. So dwarfed are we by the immensity of space and time that everything that we think, do or feel is unutterably trivial.[6] But to us it is not trivial at all. The writing of *Hamlet* may have contributed little to the universe, but it has enriched the lives of millions of people since Shakespeare's death.

It is not necessary here to embark on a detailed study of what makes a human life meaningful.[7] The important thing is that there is a relevant objective viewpoint from which lives and their contents can be assessed for their significance within a broader context, and that individuals can assume this viewpoint on their own as well as on others' lives. The availability of this point of view explains how we can take a rational self-interested concern in our posthumous future, since the contribution that our lives make to the human good may extend far beyond our lifetime. Because we want to matter to ourselves "from the outside", we care about the impact we shall make upon the lives of others although we know we shall not be around to witness it.

"No posthumous events", wrote Patrtridge, "can in any way alter a single instant of the full scope of events that constitute a completed life" (1981: 253). Posthumous events can, though, affect the meaning of those events, and this is something that concerns us as "inveterately teleological beings". The fortunes of *Hamlet* in the centuries since Shakespeare's death identify it as one of the world's most influential plays. But it could have turned out otherwise: *Hamlet* might have flopped with its first audiences and swiftly been forgotten. Such a fate would have adversely affected the meaningfulness of Shakespeare's life. And while most people have little prospect of making an impact of Shakespearean proportions on their fellow men and women, they have reason to be anxious if they anticipate that their more modest contributions may be posthumously blocked.

7 | Dealing with the dead

Are the dead ends in themselves?

It has become an ethical commonplace that we should always treat people as ends in themselves, and never merely as means (Kant 2002: §2). We satisfy Kant's resounding principle in the case of living persons by regarding them as intrinsically valuable beings who may not be treated principally as sources of advantage to ourselves. Predatory or exploitative attitudes to others are incompatible with the respect that is properly owed to their humanity. It is true, of course, that none of us could prosper or even survive without a lot of assistance from other people. But Kant's principle is not the impossible injunction to be entirely self-sufficient. Rather, we are obliged to accord importance to others' needs and interests as well as our own, and to make sure that the flow of benefits is not one-way traffic. We must be ready to give as well as take.

So much for our duty to the living. What about the dead? Do they retain the status of ends-in-themselves? Or does moral significance, or the possession of rights, cease when a person breathes her last? Living human beings are self-conscious subjects capable of leading rich and rewarding lives; dead ones are not or, it might be more pertinent to say, no longer are. Obviously our moral relations with the dead must be very different from those we have with the living. We cannot cause the dead any physical or mental pain, deceive or lie to them, disappoint or embarrass them. Nor can we bring them pleasure or give them a helping hand, or provide comfort or reassurance in times of trouble. On the other hand, when a person is dead, it is still possible for us to keep or break promises we made to her while alive, speak well or ill of her, and promote or impede the fulfilment of her wishes. There are also new *prima facie* moral obligations we incur with regard to the dead: for example, to execute the terms of their wills, and to treat their physical remains with due respect.

But are the *prima facie* duties we have towards the dead real ones? Certainly many people take them very seriously. Yet the difficulty is to see how there could be genuine moral duties towards non-existent subjects. We are back again in familiar territory. Superficially, the "moral existence condition" seems plausible:

> Nothing of moral significance can happen to a subject s at t unless s exists at t.

Unless some means can be found of refuting, or evading, this condition, the case for genuine moral duties in regard to the deceased has not been made.

It is sometimes said that the dead live on in our memories. But this notion of survival seems too metaphorical to form the basis of an argument for moral obligations to the dead, and we cannot have duties towards memories. Some writers in the social sciences have gone a step further and envisaged the dead as retaining a kind of existence on the basis of their former membership of communities that remain in being. On this account, the identities of individuals, who are pictured as atomic constituents of a social molecule, are intimately bound up with that of their societies. So closely are individual identities integrated with social ones that they effectively merge into them. Therefore, when a person dies, her identity need not die with her, since it has become incorporated within that of the broader community. In this manner, the dead retain their social linkages with others and so remain part of the moral constituency.

One of the more lucid expositions of this rather opaque thought is provided by Tarlow. In her view, "people are constituted in part by the way that they relate to others, and ... identities are formed by interactions and the understandings of others". Who and what a person is depends heavily on "the meanings, roles and expectations ascribed by others within cultural contexts". But social existence is not necessarily coeval with life. In fact, people "can and do have an existence after death", not as souls or spirits but "through their continuous creation and re-creation by people in the present". Tarlow suggests that "[o]ur practices themselves then animate the (often) forgotten dead and in one sense bring them into being". These practices include not just the efforts of scholars and researchers to uncover the reality of past lives but also the imaginative activities of "novelists and novel-readers, TV audiences, film-makers, 'descendants', museum-goers and so on" (Tarlow 1999: 201–2). As a result of all these animating processes, the dead retain a social presence and consequently a moral status.

Tarlow vividly conveys the importance that the dead can continue to have in our private and social experience. Yet, despite her best endeavours in its favour, it is not possible to accept the idea that deceased people are literally "reanimated" by any practices of the living. When we remember the dead we think of them as they were when alive but we do not suppose that our recollections restore them to life. Dead people can exercise a profound influence on the living but only through the traces they leave behind them. To speak, as Tarlow does, of a person's identity surviving her death is misleading if it is taken to mean that somehow *she* survives it. However we construe the idea of an individual's social identity, it should not be thought of as a kind of talisman keeping non-existence at bay. And while we should give due credit to the creative talents of those engaged in "animating the (often forgotten) dead", we must not confuse their achievement with a literal resurrection of the dead. Our sense of who we are is strongly bound up with our awareness of our ancestry, both genetic and cultural. The influence of our forebears is constantly felt, energizing and inescapable. But the dead are nonetheless dead, no matter how vibrantly they live in our imaginations.

It is also fallacious to argue that, as the identities of individuals merge into the identities of their societies, the continuation of the society ensures that the individual, too, in some sort continues after death. Even if the notion of merging identities could be plausibly elucidated (which is doubtful), the argument would still be objectionable. It is contradictory to hold that something that ceases to exist nevertheless continues to exist because some larger thing to which it stood in a part–whole relation remains in being. A thing either exists or it does not, and a whole that loses a part while remaining otherwise intact does not in some mystic way preserve the part.[1]

We have been looking at a line of argument that attempts to ground the moral status of the dead in a certain conception of the integrity of society. Although there are grounds for thinking that this line fails, another, very different, way of deploying an idea of social wholeness in support of the ascription of a moral standing to the dead has been defended by Partridge.

Partridge, as we have seen, denies that the dead can be genuinely harmed or benefited by anything that may happen posthumously. However, he believes that there is considerable social advantage to be gained from promoting the "fiction" that people can be harmed after death by, for example, the passing of slander, the breaking of promises made to them during life, or the flouting of their testamentary wishes. The reason, in Partridge's words, is that: "the casual slandering of reputation and breaking of promises and wills after a person's death compromise and damage the moral point of view, at enormous cost to the moral order in society and thus to the persons who live and act within the society" (1981: 258). If, for instance, Alfred Nobel's family, lacking his interests in the arts and sciences, had managed to prevent any of his legacy going to the funding of prizes in these areas, they would have wrongly violated a contract made with him during his lifetime, even though this could do him no posthumous harm (*ibid.*: 260).

But two different and incompatible ideas are running in parallel here. On the one hand, Partridge claims that, while the dead cannot be harmed by things that would be harmful to the living (e.g. acts of slander or promise-breaking), it is good to *pretend* that they can be, since this serves to sustain the "moral order" of society. If some instances of passing slander or taking promises lightly were regarded as acceptable, then general respect for the categorical imperatives to refrain from slander and to keep our promises would be undermined. On the other hand, Partridge contends that if a promise made to a living person is posthumously broken, then a *genuine* wrong has been done to the ante-mortem person. But if that is so, then the notion of the vulnerability of the dead is not a "fiction". Partridge attempts to link these ideas by suggesting that, if we saw that putative moral obligations to the dead were being blithely ignored in regard to others, we would fear that the same might happen in our own case. But this leaves the status of those putative obligations uncertain, as well as the rationality of our concern for what may happen to us after death.

The idea that it aids the moral health of society to maintain the noble fiction that the dead can be harmed faces another difficulty. Allowing that *prima facie* obligations may sometimes be broken could conceivably have a negative effect on the respect for morality. Yet if the fear is that making exceptions to general moral principles has a tendency to weaken adherence to them, one may fairly wonder whether telling this lie will not itself endanger the allegiance to veracity of those who tell it, knowing it to be untrue. A noble lie is still a lie, irrespective of its good intentions. It is paradoxical to suppose that a respect for morality can be promoted by the invention of bogus duties. If the dead are really beyond harm, it would seem more conducive to the public good to persuade people of this, so that they cease feeling anxious about their posthumous condition; that way they will become clearer, too, about the real scope of their moral obligations.

More promising is Partridge's second idea: that things can be done after a person's death that wrong the ante-mortem subject. This, of course, is an idea that we have encountered in previous chapters, and, unlike the first, it has nothing particularly to do with notions of social integrity or utility. On this account, if the executors of Nobel's will disregard his instruction to allocate funds to support a prize for literature, then they harmfully block a project of the living man. That would be wrong, since Nobel's executors have accepted an obligation to discharge his testamentary wishes. (Such obligations may be thought to lapse where a testator's wishes are immoral, illegal or otherwise unreasonable, but that cannot credibly be claimed in this case.) This diagnosis of the moral fault has the merit of being consistent with the moral existence condition. But the advantage may come at a cost. Identifying the living Nobel as the subject of the wrong satisfies the moral existence condition but sits less comfortably with our intuition that the wrong done to Nobel is not exclusively pre-posthumous. Indeed, the most natural answer to the question "When is Nobel being wronged by his executors' decision?" is: during the period in which a literature prize ought to be awarded and is not.

Once again we can look to the notion of Cambridge change and Cambridge properties to help us through the difficulty. We can say that Nobel is wronged when, by a Cambridge change, he acquires the Cambridge property of being someone whose testamentary wishes have been flouted. Admittedly, in saying this we implicitly reject the moral existence condition. But the moral existence condition *should* be rejected, because it fails to allow for the doing of wrong by the causing of morally inadmissible Cambridge changes to the dead. Applying the idea of Cambridge change enables us to explain how people can be treated morally wrongly or well even after death. And it has the advantage of doing this without relying on any thesis that the dead are still in existence, either as souls, or as memories, or as "social identities".

But we have not yet answered the more fundamental question we began with: are the dead ends in themselves, or do people lose that status when they die? I suggest that the best response to this is that we should think of people as being ends in themselves not before they die or after they die but *tout court* or timelessly. To be an end in oneself is logically rather like being a great (or a lousy) painter, or a challenging philosopher, or a person to be looked up to. If we said that Rubens was a great artist or Heidegger a difficult philosopher, we would find it disconcerting to be asked *when* Rubens was great or Heidegger difficult. In making such remarks, we are ascribing attributes timelessly to their subjects. Saying that Heidegger is difficult is not like saying that Heidegger is in his study. It is true that attributes that we timelessly ascribe generally pertain to a subject on account of temporally situated factors. Rubens is a great painter by virtue of having produced a large number of masterpieces in his career. Similarly, Rubens is an end in himself on account of the humanity he instantiated during the sixty-three years of his life. But it should not be inferred that Rubens was no longer a great painter or an end in himself after his death in 1640.

One advantage of holding that we possess the status of ends in ourselves timelessly is that it fits neatly with our disposition to think that people can be treated morally well or badly after their deaths. When, in Partridge's example, Nobel's provision for prizes in the arts is blocked by his executors, the failure to respect his autonomy is a failure to respect him. The executors' action is out of order because it is an inappropriate response to Nobel's status as an end in himself.

In *The Metaphysics of Morals*, Kant remarks that "in the context of his rights in relation to others, I actually regard every person simply in terms of his humanity". This, he insists, applies also to the dead, who continue to hold rights in virtue of their humanity. When we consider our moral obligations to deceased people, we should "abstract … from everything physical (i.e. everything belonging to their existence in space and time)" (1991: 111). Since Kant elsewhere makes clear that possessing humanity is a sufficient condition for being an end in oneself,[2] it is clear that he believes a person to be timelessly an end in himself on the basis of being timelessly human. Once an end in oneself, always an end in oneself.

Honouring the dead

If persons are timelessly ends in themselves, it follows that they should be treated as such even after death. In Kant's view, reason gives "law a priori that extends its commands and prohibitions even beyond the limits of life". Thus it would be "at least ungenerous" to slander someone after his death when he can no longer defend himself. Even though he will never be pained by learning of the slander, to besmirch his reputation is to fail to treat his humanity respectfully (Kant 1991: 111).

When loved ones die, we do not normally need to be told that we ought to honour them; this is something we do instinctively. If the commands of the moral law extend beyond death, then so too do our spontaneous affection, concern and respect. It would be hard, if not impossible, to cancel the feelings that we have for living persons as soon as they die. The duty to show honour to our dead is therefore not one that is exacted from us reluctantly, like loving our enemies or paying our taxes. We are also inclined to take it very ill if others do not show a proper respect for their memory.

One of the more obvious ways in which we express our love and respect for the dead is via funerals and mourning rites. For hygienic and aesthetic reasons corpses need to be removed from the presence of the living, yet a funeral is a great deal more than an exercise in waste-disposal. Although funerals and exequies have taken vastly different forms in different cultures, they typically deploy symbols intended to represent the passing of a person as a significant event not just for the individual but for his family, friends and community. Funerals are a way of emphasizing that a person's death matters because his life has done so. They can be thought of as rites of passage, marking the transition of the deceased person from one status to another. They are also rites of passage for those who remain behind, helping them to adjust emotionally, spiritually and practically to life without the deceased. Funerals can also help to restore dignity to the dead where the process of dying has been undignified.

In *The City of God*, Augustine emphasized the social dimension of funerals, holding that they were rather "solaces to the living, than furtherances to the dead" (book I, ch. 12; 1945: vol. 1, 16). No actual harm would come to the soul of a Christian who had not been buried with proper Christian rites. It made no difference to one's eligibility for heaven, claimed Augustine, whether one's remains finished up in a marble tomb or a beast's belly. Nevertheless, he conceded that it goes against the grain, both morally and sentimentally, to be careless about our own dead bodies or about those of people we love:

> For if the garment or ring of one's father be so much the more esteemed of his posterity, by how much they held him dearer in their affection; then are not our bodies to be despised, seeing that we wear them more near unto our-selves than any attire whatsoever. For these are no part of external ornament or assistance unto man, but of his express nature. (*Ibid.*)

Hence the funerals of the righteous have customarily been performed "with a zealous care" and suitable monuments to their memory provided (book I, ch. 12; 1945: vol. 1, 17). As a modern writer on funerals and their meanings notes, in our more secular age we still like to express the respect and allegiance we feel towards the dead through ceremonies and memorials. "Whether through gravestones, remains cast to the wind or through woodland burial," writes Douglas Davies, "we find human beings relating to their dead". Indeed, "[b]eing the embodied creatures we are, the 'place' of memory may be none other than ourselves", the quick being living reminders, by their inherited features and resemblances, of the dead (Davies 2005: 130).

A funeral, however important as a rite of passage and a ceremonious leave-taking, is soon over; memories of the dead person last very much longer. We have looked at some of the reasons why people might wish to be remembered after their deaths. However, there can be exceptions. Someone who expects to be remembered badly might prefer not to be remembered at all. So, for a very different reason, might a person who fears that his passing will cause those who survive him excessive grief. In Sonnet 71, Shakespeare, or his poetic persona, requests:

> When I perhaps compounded am with clay,
> Do not so much as my poor name rehearse,
> But let your love even with my life decay.

There may be an element of poetic hyperbole here; probably rather few of us would be content to be remembered by those who care for us only so long as they hear "the surly sullen bell" warn that we have gone "with vilest worms to dwell". A "love" that can be switched off so quickly could hardly have been the genuine article in the first place. Yet love sits uneasily with complacency about the pain that one's death will produce. The tension between one's natural wish to be affectionately remembered and one's equally natural desire not to cause one's loved ones distress is an important, if often overlooked, aspect of the painfulness of dying.[3]

Until around a hundred years ago, it was common for gravestones and memorials to supply elaborate lists of the achievements and merits of the deceased. Having one's virtues inscribed in stone or bronze for all to see must have seemed a very good way of being favourably remembered long after one had gone to dwell with the worms. The downside of the practice was that the fulsomeness of many such testimonials undermined confidence in their veracity, and they increasingly came to be seen as mere formal exercises in piety. In a more laconic age (or when scepticism could stand the strain no longer) the fashion for such commemorations declined. But it would be unduly cynical to suppose that the custom of memorializing the dead as paragons was rooted entirely in the desire for self-advertisement or family pride. It probably owed something too to the longstanding tradition that the dead should be spoken of respectfully: a tradition encapsulated in the old Latin tag *de mortuis nihil nisi bene* (say nothing but good things about the dead). Although this principle stops short of enjoining us to tell flattering lies about the dead, it is not a principle of candour, since it calls on us to be economical with the truth and to pass over in silence things that discredit them.

The *de mortuis* principle, as I shall call it, was ascribed by Diogenes Laertius to the Lacedaemonian sage Chilo (or Chilone), and it was defended by many classical writers, including Cicero and Cato the Younger (*Lives of the Philosphers*, book 1, "Chilo"). Part of its initial attractiveness doubtless stems from a sense that revealing an uncomplimentary fact about someone who cannot respond is like kicking a man when he's down. Our sense of fair play persuades us that people should have the chance to reply to negative things that are said about them. This is not a matter just of good manners but of good morals. Our courts of law allow accused individuals the opportunity to speak in their own behalf even where there is compelling evidence of their guilt.

One might have expected the *de mortuis* principle to appeal to Kant, who, we saw, thought it "ungenerous to spread reproaches against one who is absent and cannot defend himself". However, Kant believed that while it was ungenerous to slander a dead person, "a well-founded accusation against him is still in order (so that the principle *de mortuis nihil nisi bene* is incorrect)" (1991: 111). For Kant, generosity to the dead should not be at the expense of truthfulness. While the slanderer breaks the moral law by telling lies, the person who brings "a well-founded accusation" against another shows a robust respect for veracity. But we need not suppose that Kant would have approved of randomly raking up discreditable facts about the dead. To set ourselves up as recording angels with the role of disclosing all that we can discover to the discredit of others, whether dead or alive, would be the height of arrogant self-righteousness. There are times when we should "tell the truth and shame the devil", but we ought not to become morally officious busybodies.

Kant's rejection of the *de mortuis* principle is importantly in keeping with his advocacy of treating people as ends. One theme running through his ethical writings is that we show proper respect for other human beings only if we take them seriously as moral agents. We should look on ourselves and others as rationally able to determine moral requirements and to act autonomously on the basis of those determinations. Having this capacity, human beings should be held morally responsible for their acts, because the moral law is the practical law governing the mutual relations between persons (the members of the "kingdom of ends") and human beings are dignified, above all, by their exercise of rational moral agency. To turn a blind eye to what people do as moral agents is to disregard the main basis of their dignity; it also shows a culpable lack of concern for the effects of their actions on other ends-in-themselves. Whitewashing moral agents is *not* a way of respecting them.

Although we should not forget to remove the beam from our own eye before we censure the mote in our brother's, it is neither honest nor sensible to pretend that others have no faults. The kingdom of ends is a community of agents capable of doing good and evil deeds, not a mutual admiration society. And as the dead are timelessly members of the kingdom of ends, they, too, deserve to be treated as agents whose acts were and remain morally significant. Since they cannot defend themselves, it is imperative that we should make sure of our facts before making charges. Accusations against the dead, as Kant says, need to be well-founded. But where they are, it may be more respectful to bring than to suppress them.

It would be difficult to draw up hard and fast rules as to when, by whom and to whom discreditable truths should, or may, be revealed. Taking the dead seriously as moral agents does not mean that their every peccadillo should be advertised to the widest possible public. We can avoid whitewashing the dead without shouting their dispraises from the rooftop. The latter is disrespectful because it demeans individuals to represent them as being morally answerable to all and sundry. There can be legitimate public and private interests in learning the truth about the dead but there is no universal right to be told the guilty secrets of people whose lives have never impinged on our own, or to sit in judgement on them. (From this point of view, those who have deliberately placed themselves in the public eye may have less right to immunity from media attention or the "picklocks of biographers"; but mere prurient poking into their private lives serves no defensible purpose.)

Those who reveal or publicize the faults and failings of other people often do so for reasons that have nothing to do with respect but are the fruit of malice, envy, jealousy, contempt, self-righteousness and a host of other disreputable motives. That the charges they bring are true does not change the fact that they are prompted by a bad will. But the fact that something may be done from a bad motive does not entail that it can never be done from a good one. In some cases it would be absurd, even dangerous, to overlook or attempt to disguise others' faults. Someone who talked only about the benefits that Hitler brought to Germany and ignored all the bad things he did would be a pernicious moral influence as well as an unreliable historian. Standing up for one's own moral principles is incompatible with scrupulously refraining from criticism of those who break them. It would be bad for the moral health of the kingdom of ends if everyone abstained, from modesty or a misplaced sense of charity, from judging others.

Treating the dead with the respect they deserve as members of the kingdom of ends requires, then, taking them seriously as moral agents. Yet doing this can be difficult where time and change have placed obstacles in the way of our imaginative access to other lives. Because the past is a distant country where things are done differently, it can be hard to obtain a three-dimensional sense of past individuals. And since our knowledge of the inscape of particular lives is so limited, the temptation is to think of the dead in generalized categories, as medieval monks, feudal peasants, domestic servants, crusading knights, Egyptian nobles and so on. (We often do the same in regard to our contemporaries too, but at least here our prejudices and oversimplifications are open to correction by experience.) A further problem we face in framing moral judgements about past people is that moral standards vary over time. There has never been a universally accepted conception of the good moral agent. One age or culture's paragon is another's prig, or even pariah. The judgements we make of past people on the basis of our modern moral standards may be markedly out of line with those that would have been made in their own day. Since people can only judge by the standards available to them, our judgements need to take this into account or risk being unfair. Even if a person's conscience is, in Richard Arneson's vivid metaphor, a "broken thermometer" (1999: 120–21), it is still the only device she has for taking the moral temperature.

If anachronism is one potential pitfall when we seek to pass moral judgement on former people, another is the temptation to view the past over-romantically, through rose-tinted spectacles. (While there is nothing very new about this temptation, it has received a boost from the advent of the "heritage" industry and the conception of history as theme-park.) As a result, moral judge-ments become distorted by our love of the exciting and exotic, and we may find ourselves making excuses for men and women who did morally monstrous things. Although people are rightly held to be innocent until proved guilty, there is nothing admirable about concocting ingenious excuses for some of history's more colourful villains. (Examples are likely to be contentious, but I would tenta-tively propose Genghis Khan and King Richard III as recent unde-serving beneficiaries of such favourable treatment.) Justice does not cease to matter simply because the subjects of appraisal are dead. Judging people of the past is not an intellectual game, in which we display our cleverness at overturning well-founded accusations. We show proof of our sense of civilized values when we try to get those judgements right.

Using human remains: the case of archaeology

Is it wrong, or disrespectful, to utilize the physical remains of deceased people for our own purposes? In some cases, surely not. Some people carry donor cards permitting their organs to be used posthumously for transplant surgery, while others bequeath their bodies to medical research. Since they consent to the use of their bodies or bodily parts after death, there is not even a *prima facie* case for saying that such treatment is incompatible with their sta-tus as ends in themselves. In contrast, there is a strong *prima facie* case for asserting that people are illegitimately treated merely as means when their remains are taken for research or other purposes without their consent.

One context in which this commonly happens – and the one that we shall take for our case study – is that of archaeological research. Typically archaeologists uncover in the name of science the remains of people who have not anticipated such disturbance and who would probably have refused their consent to it if they had. Until quite recently many researchers appear not even to have grasped that there might be ethical issues here. Bodily remains were too often regarded not as the remnants of people who once lived and breathed as we do, but merely as "data", devoid of ethical sig-nificance. Recent years have seen a growing awareness by members of the archaeological and kindred professions that human remains should be treated with a measure of respect. One influential ethical code, the Vermillion Accord on Human Remains, adopted by the World Archaeological Congress at its meeting in Vermillion, South Dakota, in 1989, laid down, among other things, that:

1. Respect for the mortal remains of the dead shall be accorded to all, irrespective of race, religion, nationality, custom and tradition;
2. Respect for the wishes of the dead concerning disposition shall be accorded wherever possible, reasonable and lawful, when they can be known or reasonably inferred.[4]

One problem with these and other similar statements is that they are too vague to yield much practical guidance. What exactly does it mean to "show respect" to the remains of the dead, as the first Vermillion principle enjoins us? Some cultural traditions look on *any* interference with remains as disrespectful. To defer to this hard-line position would rule out much archaeological activity immediately. Even among Western-trained archaeologists themselves, views differ as to what respectful treatment of remains requires, with some holding that "showing respect" involves no more than not treating bones or body parts as junk or comic props or curios. On a more rigorous view, respecting remains precludes not just irreverent handling of them but also all unnecessary disturbance, and demands the restoration or reburial of all but the most crucially significant remains at the end of a research project.

The notion of respecting the *wishes* of the dead, referred to in the second Vermillion principle, at first sight leaves rather less room for interpretation. Normally, the only way to respect a person's wishes is by following them. If someone said to you, "I respect your wish that I should turn down my radio/keep off your lawn/go to church on Sundays, but I'm not going to fall in with it", you would conclude that he did not really respect your wish at all. Archaeologists may not always know just how the owners of remains would have responded to the prospect of disturbance. But often enough is known about the cultural background of their subjects for a reliable guess to be hazarded that they would have been unhappy with it. If researchers still proceed to tamper with tombs or grave sites, this might seem to be a clear breach of the second Vermillion principle. But that principle contains a get-out clause. It asserts that the known or "reasonably inferred" wishes of the dead concerning the treatment of their remains should be respected *wherever this is "possible" or "reasonable"*. Archaeologists could therefore claim – justifiably, from their point of view – that it was neither "possible" nor "reasonable" to desist from intrusive investigation of bodies or burials where this promised to yield data vital to their research projects. The subjects whose remains they disturb might well have had quite different ideas about what was possible or reasonable. The question is whose possibility and whose reasonableness is to count.

Consider a man, Theseus, who is very anxious that his body should remain undisturbed after it has been buried in a sacred place according to the customary rites of his society. Theseus's anxiety could stem from one or more of several sources: a fear that such disturbance would prevent his spirit finding rest; a desire that his privacy or his dignity should be posthumously maintained; a conviction that tampering with his remains is sacrilegious; or a dislike of those remains being utilized in the service of alien interests. If, centuries later, archaeologists exhume his skeleton and remove it, along with his grave goods, to a laboratory for detailed examination, they do so against the wishes of the ante-mortem subject. Suppose, too, that the researchers know enough about the culture of the people they are studying to be able to infer with reasonable certainty that in tampering with Theseus's skeleton they are acting against its owner's wishes. Are these archaeologists doing wrong?

They might say in their defence that they are only handling bones, and that bones, being inanimate, are not things that can be harmed or wronged. But this would be a weak response. It is not the bones to which offence – if offence there is – is being done, but Theseus.[5] Alternatively, they might claim that they would not have disturbed the remains if there had been any reasonable alternative method of procuring the data they required. Unfortunately, even if this plea is sincere, it begs the crucial question about whether their or their subject's interests should take priority. If they are philosophically minded, they might suggest that no real harm or wrong can be done to a person who no longer exists. But the rejoinder to this is that people can be harmed or wronged posthumously by changes of a Cambridge kind. When the archaeologists go to work, Theseus undergoes two pertinent Cambridge changes: from being a person whose remains lie untouched in the grave to one whose remains no longer lie there, and from being someone whose wishes for those remains have been followed to someone whose wishes have been flouted. Although these changes are Cambridge rather than "real", this is no reason, if our earlier arguments were correct, to regard them as morally irrelevant.

The first change could, admittedly, be argued to be morally neutral if it were false that people suffer genuine harm when their bodily remains or burials are disturbed. But the second is a different case. A modern researcher might be dismissive of some of Theseus's reasons for not wanting his remains to be disturbed (e.g. his belief that such disturbance will cause his ghost to be troubled). Yet to disregard his wishes on this basis would be to miss the main point. A person may reasonably be ascribed an interest in making for himself the crucial decisions that (he takes to) determine his fate or fortune. This is the interest thought important enough to be enshrined in the Fourteenth Amendment to the US Constitution, which, in the words of a recent Supreme Court ruling, takes "matters involving the most intimate and personal choices a person may make in his lifetime, choices central to a person's dignity and autonomy", to be his business and his alone.[6] And what, after all, could be more "intimate and personal" than the decision about how one wants one's remains disposed of? Disregarding without very good reason a person's most heartfelt wishes for himself is disrespectful to him as a rational, self-determining being.[7] While indecent or impractical requests for the disposal of bodily remains may legitimately be ignored (for instance, someone has no right to insist that his body should be eaten by his heirs, or that his ashes should be scattered at the North Pole), the default position should be one of compliance.

Should archaeologists therefore adopt a working maxim of "when in doubt, stay out"? (Could archaeology even survive as a major social science if they did?) Or are there any arguments that might warrant a more liberal and permissive policy with regard to archaeological disturbance of the dead?

It is worth, to begin with, reminding ourselves that former people are not the only bearers of morally relevant interests. Currently living people, including practising archaeologists, have morally significant interests too. Furthermore, in recent decades, representatives of indigenous peoples in North America, Australia, New Zealand

and elsewhere have become more forceful than previously in their demands that archaeological and anthropological research should be responsible not just to scientific imperatives but to the ethical imperative to respect alternative cultural traditions. Many of these traditions are deeply opposed to any interference with ancestral graves or sacred sites, and legislation in a number of countries (of which the 1990 Native American Graves Protection and Repatriation Act in the USA is the best-known example) has placed tight restrictions on the activities of archaeologists. The third principle of the Vermillion Accord holds that "respect for the wishes of the local community and or relatives and guardians of the dead shall be accorded whenever possible, reasonable and lawful". There are thus three distinguishable sets of moral stakeholders in the archaeological enterprise: researchers (and their audience), the dead themselves and their genetic or cultural descendants.

It would be a mistake, though, to suppose that the interests of these three groups are always entirely discrete. Descendants of the subjects of archaeological research often see themselves as guardians of the dead (whom they may regard as retaining a presence as spirit members of the community). But they may also themselves take an interest in the research being carried out, particularly where archaeologists have taken the trouble to discuss their purposes, methods and results with the local community. In the USA there has been rapid growth in research projects involving close cooperation between archaeologists and local people, where the ethical approval of the latter is sought before any intrusive excavations or other procedures are carried out, and where the pooling of scientific and traditional knowledge enables a richer picture of the past to emerge than would be likely to issue from the unaided efforts of the former.

By working in close association with members of communities who may have a considerably better idea of what the subjects of the research would or would not have tolerated than they can frame from their external viewpoint, archaeologists reduce the risk of morally offending against the dead. Further, it is often possible to take a light-touch approach to excavation without seriously jeopardizing the prospect of obtaining the desired scientific data. For example, an archaeological team wishing to excavate an important cemetery in a sensitive area might reach an agreement with the local people that only a small section of the site should be disturbed, under the supervision of community representatives, and that the minimum of damage should be done and the maximum of respect be paid to the uncovered remains. In that way the interests of the living parties and of the dead receive consideration, but no single party's interests dominate.

In the past few years the stereotypical view of archaeology as focused on the advancement of knowledge has been tempered by an increasing tendency to look on its practitioners as stewards of the archaeological record. Archaeologists who see themselves in a custodial role, responsible for protecting and preserving materials *in situ* along with collections and records, are, one would hope, less likely than those who do not to engage in unnecessarily destructive or intrusive fieldwork. They will apply a principle of diminishing marginal returns and avoid exhuming a hundred skeletons where a small number will supply most of the information they need. In this way, they can justifiably claim to be stewards serving the interests not only of present and future generations but of past ones too.

Finally, there is a reply of a different kind to the objection that exhumation of the dead, even where practised on the most minimal scale consistent with the achievement of reasonable research objectives, will tend to conflict with the interests of the subjects concerned. If archaeologists exploit the remains of the dead, it is possible to argue that they do one thing for them in return. Recall Browne's observation that "Oblivion is a kind of Annihilation, and for things to be as though they had not been is like unto never being" (1969: 242). Archaeology is one – highly effective – way of keeping in mind the reality of past lives, and so, arguably, of holding absurdity at bay. It is a plausible claim that the revelations by archaeologists of the details of past lives are a stronger counter to oblivion than the preservation of dead bodies intact in their graves. Theseus would not relish the thought of some future archaeologist measuring his cranial capacity or extracting DNA from his bone marrow but, just conceivably, he might find it an acceptable price to pay for a degree of posthumous remembrance. So if oblivion is itself a form of indignity, we may be forced to take a more subtle view of the bearing of archaeology on the dignity of the ante-mortem subjects of its researches. Some of those subjects might have preferred to be recalled via the examination of their burials than to lie forever forgotten; although admittedly we cannot know which these are.[8]

Therefore we should not be too quick to assume that archaeological disturbance of the dead always disserves its subjects. Even
if it sometimes does, there are other relevant interests than need
to be weighed alongside those of past people. To refuse to conduct
investigations that disturb human remains could be held to harm
living people who see knowledge about the past as a valuable good;
they too are ends in themselves with interests that matter. Nevertheless, it is hard to see by what neutral standard these potentially
conflicting interests could be weighed against one another. And
without such a yardstick to determine which, or whose, interests
carry the more weight in cases of conflict, the decisions arrived at
will inevitably involve a degree of arbitrariness. Yet if the eternal
triangle linking researchers, the dead people they study and their
living descendants will never be an easy one either practically or
ethically, it is wrong to think of their interests as invariably conflicting and irreconcilable. Archaeologists who operate in a spirit of
stewardship can show respect to the dead without greatly compro-
mising their professional concerns. The dead need not be thought
of as being either morally off-limits to archaeologists, or as a morally unproblematic research resource to whose remnants anything
may be done. The truth, as so often where interests compete, lies
somewhere between the extremes.

And finally ...

O, but they say the tongues of dying men
Enforce attention like deep harmony.
Where words are scarce, they are seldom spent in vain;
For they breathe truth that breathe their words in pain.
He that no more must say is listen'd more
Than they whom youth and ease have taught to glose;
More are men's ends mark'd than their lives before.

(*King Richard II* II.1.5–11)

There is a well-entrenched tradition that people who die in their
beds, with the opportunity to reflect on their experience to date,
are in an epistemically privileged position to "cast a cold eye on life,
on death", and to say some wise words for the benefit of those left

behind. Shakespeare's dying duke John of Gaunt certainly seems to have accepted this view (though the sermon that he delivers to the wayward King Richard falls on deaf ears). Although no one, as Heidegger has emphasized, can step outside her life and see it whole, those who know they are close to death can make the nearest approach to the comprehensive view. If Solon's claim (as quoted by Aristotle) is true that no man should be called *eudaimon* before his death, people who have only days or hours to live are closest to being able to judge whether or not they have led happy and successful lives.

It is sometimes thought that death-bed reflections and last words carry a special kind of authority, issuing as they do from a unique (literally, once in a lifetime) perspective. But this has also been doubted. Robert Kastenbaum remarks that though "wise people may have wise things to say as they near the end of their lives, it is possible that foolish, boring, and neurotic people stay in character by saying foolish, boring, and neurotic things" (1993: 281–2). Moreover physical and mental ill-health may impair the capacity for lucid thought of even the wisest people, whilst evasive strategies may be adopted to distance the decedent from the thought of impending death.[9] The dislike of leaving loose ends can also prompt dying people to pay a surprising amount of attention to matters that may appear trivial in the greater scheme of things. Socrates' last words were an instruction to Criton to pay a cock that was owed to Asclepius, the god of healing (Plato, *Phaedo*, 118a; 1956b: 521); a dying woman of my acquaintance requested her son to ensure that accounts were settled with the milkman.

Montaigne likewise thought that outstanding wisdom or virtue could not be expected from dying people who had shown few signs of them during life. "I always interpret a man's death," he wrote, "by his life. And if I am given an account of an apparently strong death linked to a weakling life, I maintain that it was produced by some weakling cause in keeping with that life" (1987: 476). For instance, what may at first appear to be admirable resignation to the inevitable sometimes turns out to be merely the insensibility of the moribund. Genuinely good fruit comes only from good trees. The prospect of death can serve to concentrate the mind, but it cannot instil wisdom or virtue when those qualities were previously absent.

Although we are unlikely to produce any unwonted, out-of-character pearls of wisdom when nearing our end, we are still in the best position we shall ever be in to survey our career as a whole, with a lifetime's experience behind us. But engaging in such a retrospective exercise can be an unnerving experience and a source of existential anxiety. What if we should find (or think we have found) that we have lived absurdly, got our priorities wrong, made poor choices, failed to fulfil ourselves? It is too late now to do anything about our unrealized hopes, our failures and under-achievements, our misadventures and wasted chances! The only saving grace is that we won't need to worry about them for very much longer.

A humorist once remarked, "When you open a can of worms, you cannot expect butterflies to fly out". Fortunately, most lives are not cans of worms. But nor do most contain only butterflies. It may therefore appear more prudent to keep the lid on the can. Self-examination is a salutary exercise when it promotes self-improvement but this requires time that the dying do not have. If we realise our failings when it is too late to remedy them, we appear to have disturbed our peace of mind to no useful purpose. To follow the Socratic maxim "Know yourself" is, at this stage, to be asking for trouble. Would it not be better to die in blissful ignorance of our failures and shortcomings than in a state of bitter and impotent regret for them?

I suspect that very few people would answer this question affirmatively. In part this may reflect the difficulty that we have in taking seriously the fact that we shall die. Since we can scarcely imagine the tomorrow that will dawn without us it is hard to believe that it is ever too late to put right what we see to be wrong. But most people seem not much attracted by the thought of attempting such blatant self-deception at what they know to be (their imaginative limitations notwithstanding) the supreme crisis point of their lives. Maybe they fear the alienating effect of trying to pull the wool over their eyes at such a juncture; or perhaps they are concerned that their good points will also disappear behind the veil of ignorance. It may be relevant, too, that there are strong cultural traditions of death-bed honesty, often (as in the Christian case) grounded in ideas about the proper preparation of the soul or spirit for death. Even where belief in the underlying religious doctrines has faded, the lingering influence of such traditions can still be potent.[10]

Of course, unless we have spent our lives very ill or been especially unlucky in our circumstances, our death-bed review should reveal not only faults and failings but much in which to take satisfaction. It is true that many of the things we look back on with pleasure will not make a major impact on human affairs; yet we should beware, when standing on the brink of eternity, of undervaluing the small-scale, everyday concerns that make up much of the substance of a human life. Although we may reasonably wish to leave some significant traces that endure beyond our own temporal limits, it would be wrong to think that the only valuable lives are those that are full of vivid and memorable achievement. An important measure of success is that a life should express its owner's own values, interests, aspirations, commitments and tastes: in short, her individuality. One may not have been a great statesman or written moving plays or discovered a cure for cancer yet may nonetheless have succeeded in living the life that one intended to live, or some approximation to it. It is something if one can say (or sing) at the end, like Frank Sinatra, "I did it my way".[11]

The death of any human being is a momentous event, both objectively and subjectively. It is the end of one's own story and the beginning of a new chapter in others'. Even if one's death-bed review reveals that one's life has been quite average and ordinary – as most lives, by definition, are – one may be consoled by the reflection that one was still, in Dworkin's phrase, "a masterpiece of nature". And that is not a bad thought with which to face eternity.

Notes

Chapter 1: The nature of death

1. Cf. Jean-Paul Sartre: death is "a permanent limit of my projects" (*Being and Nothingness*, H. E. Barnes (trans.) [New York: Washington Square Press, 1966], 699–700).

2. Johnson was in fact the author of the appeal.

3. It is worth remarking that authentic choices can sometimes be of questionable wisdom. Mr Stephens, in Kazuo Ishiguro's novel *The Remains of the Day* (New York: Knopf, 1989), carefully plans his life around the dominant but highly constricting project of being an excellent butler. Authenticity is more plausibly regarded as necessary than as sufficient for living a good life. (For an incisive discussion of Mr Stephens's predicament, see Kwame Anthony Appiah, *The Ethics of Identity* [Princeton, NJ: Princeton University Press, 2005], 9–13.)

4. For a summary of the present state of opinion and further references, see M. Potts & W. D. Evans, "Does it Matter that Organ Donors are not Dead? Ethical and Policy Implications", *Journal of Medical Ethics* 31 (2005), 406–9.

5. For some further support for the idea that death may not always be instantaneous, see Steven Luper, "Posthumous Harm", *American Philosophical Quarterly* 41 (2004), 63–72, esp. 64.

6. Hume's citing of revelation as a source of support is somewhat disingenuous, since he was privately indisposed to accept it.

7. The notion that death could be good for us has raised not just the eyebrows but the hackles of some recent philosophers. Thus McMahan describes Socrates as "prating" about his hopes for the next life and considers Plato and others who have advanced such arguments to be engaging in a tawdry "strategy of denial" of death. When we look to great thinkers of the past to tell us the truth about death, what we too often find instead is "a dreary record of evasion and sophistry" (*The Ethics of Killing: Killing at the Margins of Life* [Oxford: Oxford University Press, 2002], 96). Bertrand Russell was similarly unimpressed by Socrates' final scene: "His courage in the face of death would have been more remarkable if he had not believed that he was going to enjoy eternal bliss in the company of the gods" (*History of Western Philosophy* [London: Allen and Unwin, 1946], 164).

8. See, for example, Donald Davidson, "Laws and Causes", *Dialectica* **49** (1995), 263-79.

9. Plato's argument is delivered over several pages of the *Phaedo*, starting from around 95c (*Phaedo*, in *Great Dialogues of Plato*, W. H. D. Rouse [trans.], 460–521 [New York and Toronto: New American Library, 1956], 500ff.). It is noteworthy that Plato also inherited Pythagoras's belief in the pre-existence of souls before they entered human bodies.

Chapter 2: Existential perspectives

1. Edwards is commenting not on the gospel parable but on a related scriptural passage: "Boast not thyself of tomorrow: for thou knowest not what a day may bring forth" (Proverbs 27:1).

2. At least in countries where cricket is played.

3. "The world is the content of my consciousness. I am the center, the audience for the show" (Herbert Fingarette, *Death: Philosophical Soundings* [Chicago, IL: Open Court, 1996], 83).

4. It is in principle possible that two authentic, self-creating persons could turn out to be quite similar to each other, and this would not detract from their individual value provided that the resemblance was accidental (and not the result, say, of one of them imitating the other).

5. Compare with these claims of Heidegger the strikingly modern-sounding remark of Montaigne: "We do not know where death awaits us: so let us wait for it everywhere. To practise death is to practise freedom" ("To Philosophize is to Learn How to Die", in *The Complete Essays*, M. A. Screech (ed. and trans.) [Harmondsworth: Penguin, 1987], 96).

6. It is a sobering thought that each year there is in the calendar a day that marks the *pre*-anniversary of our death, in just the way that our birthday marks the anniversary of our birth. If we knew when our "deathday" fell, we could count off the remaining years of our life. Fortunately, we do not.

7. She goes on to suggest that it is women, in particular, who have had their being-towards-death changed by their experience of being with the dying, as it is primarily "feminine being [that] has been ascribed the role of caring for the dying and grieving for the dead" (Linnell Secomb, "Philosophical Deaths and Feminine Fortitude", *Mortality* **4** [1999], 111–25, esp. 114). This seems to me (from my male standpoint) to involve a very questionable stereotyping of men's and women's relations to the dying. Many men as well as women have experience of caring for the dying, and both genders are equally capable of grieving for the dead (which in any case is oddly described as a "role"). A question is also begged by Secomb's subsequent remark that "Hegel's and Heidegger's abstractions are founded on a limited masculine understanding of and experience of death" (*ibid.*, 123).

8. See also Chapter 1 above, p. 19.

9. Taylor's denigration of life brings to mind Macbeth's "tale/ Told by an idiot, full of sound and fury,/ Signifying nothing" (V.5.29–31).

10. Tristan's words are: "Were mighty Death to stand here now, threatening both my life and my limbs, trying to will me to love no longer, how could he ever hope to destroy the love that I harbour?" (R. Wagner, *Tristan und Isolde*, S. Robb [trans.] [New York: G. Schirmer, 1965], 18).

11. Cooper quotes Anthony Kenny, "Wittgenstein's Meaning of Life", *Times Higher Education Supplement*, 19 May 1989.

Chapter 3: Long lives, short lives

1. Some rather similar sentiments have been expressed by Jonathan Glover. "Given the company of the right people", he writes, "I would be glad of the chance to sample a few million years and see how it went" (*Causing Death and Saving Lives* [Harmondsworth: Penguin, 1977], 57).

2. Steven Luper remarks that he finds Unamuno's "adamancy refreshing" (*Invulnerability* [Chicago, IL: Open Court, 1996], 104).

3. The question of why we have asymmetrical attitudes to the thought of our pre-natal non-existence (which does not worry us) and to that of our posthumous non-existence (which worries many people a great deal) is one that we shall return to in Chapter 5.

4. "If youth only knew, if old age were only capable". This saying, in its French form, can be traced back to Henri Estienne's *Les Premices, ou le livre des proverbes epigrammatisez, ou des epigrammes proverbialez* (Geneva: H. Estienne, 1594), 173.

5. There is an echo of Shakespeare in Sigmund Freud: "The value of transitoriness is a scarcity value within Time. Limits on the opportunity for pleasure heighten its preciousness" (Freud quoted in Fingarette, *Death: Philosophical Soundings*, 155).

6. Among the writers who have defended a position along these lines are John Martin Fischer, "Introduction", in *The Metaphysics of Death*, J. M. Fischer (ed.), 1–30 [Stanford, CA: Stanford University Press, 1993], 12 and McMahan, *The Ethics of Killing*, 102–3.

7. The explanation of McMahan's silence on this point is probably that he believes that the preservation of personal identity *is* compatible with such psychological changes (*The Ethics of Killing*, 102).

8. The metaphor of lives as narratives has been developed by a number of writers including Alasdair MacIntyre, *After Virtue* (London: Duckworth, 1985), ch. 15; J. David Velleman, "Well-being and Time", in Fischer (ed.), *The Metaphysics of Death*, 48–77 and "Narrative Explanation", *Philosophical Review* 112 (2003), 1–26; John Martin Fischer, "Free Will, Death and Immortality: The Role of Narrative", *Philosophical Papers* 34 (2005), 379–403.

9. In view of the secular perspective of this book, I shall not delve into the question of whether any religious conception of eternal life might be more appealing than the "worldly" versions I have looked at. But a few remarks are in order. The cruder conceptions of paradise that represent it as a kind of up-market holiday resort are open to the same Williams-style objections that life in such an environment would eventually, and maybe quite soon, become tedious. More spiritual versions are harder to evaluate. Aquinas wrote that "Final and perfect happiness can consist in nothing else than the vision of the divine essence" (*Summa Theologica*, Fathers of the English Dominican Province (trans.), 3 vols [New York: Benziger Brothers, 1947], 1a.2ae.3.8; vol. 1, 601.) I have no idea what it would be like to enjoy the beatific vision of God for all eternity. Perhaps one should think of this as being like the most beautiful experience one has ever had, only far, far better still. But could this (or any) exquisite enjoyment

be kept up for eternity? Moreover, if existence in heaven were to be fulfilling, would one not have to be active rather than merely passive? Relatedly, we might ask whether there would be any opportunities for development, or a sense that one's existence was going somewhere, in heaven. It may be suggested that one's primary heavenly "activity" would be the worshipping of God. However, it is hard to conceive this *now* as an attractive way of spending eternity unless we also envisage our desires undergoing some very profound changes; which leads to some doubt whether the second of Williams's two conditions would be satisfied. This problem will remain if we suppose, more radically, that time is experienced differently in heaven, or that heavenly experience might be wholly atemporal. But at this point the philosopher runs out of resources to pursue the question any further.

Chapter 4: Facing death

1. The last of these metaphors was used by the psychiatrist Timothy Leary during his final illness (cited in Leming & Dickinson, *Understanding Dying*, 59). Leming & Dickinson also engagingly remark that "we do not die in America; we simply take a long nap" (*ibid.*: 58).

2. Canon Henry Scott-Holland, "Death is Nothing at all", from his sermon "The King of Terrors" delivered in St Paul's Cathedral in 1910 while the body of King Edward VII was lying in state in Westminster Abbey. I am grateful to the Reverend Anthony Bash for reminding me of this poem, which, he informs me, people often ask to be read at funerals. Fortunately, poetical attempts at death denial are not always so bathetic as this, as John Donne's famous sonnet "Death be not Proud" and George Herbert's "Death" amply demonstrate.

3. All too many philosophers, McMahan thinks, have indulged in "the practice of wringing a meager drop of consolation from the rags of bad argument" (*The Ethics of Killing*, 96).

4. For one moving account of a Stoic death, see letter 77 in Seneca, *Letters from a Stoic*, selected by Robin Campbell (trans.) (Harmondsworth: Penguin, 1969), 126–7.

5. Note that while I can only fear things that are fearful or frightening to me, I can fear *that* certain things will be thus and so that I expect to be bad or painful for others rather than myself (e.g. "I fear that you will one day regret those badly chosen words").

6. The addition of the phrase within parentheses is to keep in mind the point made in Chapter 2 that some people may prefer even an irretrievably painful existence to no existence at all. (We might call this the "Belial perspective", after Milton's fallen angel: see p. 29).

7. Until the time of the Reformation, scenes of the Last Judgement ("Doom paintings") formed the standard decoration of chancel arches of parish churches throughout the length and breadth of England. The dismaying impact that these lurid visions must have had on ordinary people is difficult now to imagine. By the end of the Middle Ages the predominant opinion among theologians and religious teachers was that, in view of our natural sinfulness, only a very small proportion of mankind would be saved. To many Christians of the period it must have seemed that their mode of being was being-towards-hell.

8. This opinion may be controversial. Rai Gaita thinks it possible that some ani-

mals can have "knowledge in the shadow of death" (*The Philosopher's Dog* [London: Routledge, 2004], 70–72). He quotes J. N. Coetzee's description of the symptoms of terror shown by the dogs in a dogs' shelter when some of their number have been put down (out of sight, but possibly not out of smell). I am not convinced that this is good evidence that the dogs have knowledge of their own mortality even at that limited point in time, although they clearly know that something unusual and frightening is going on. One might, of course, ascribe "fear of death" to even quite lowly animals if one means by the phrase no more than instinctive or reflex avoidance of life-threatening situations. Amélie Rorty notes that talk about fear of death can refer to "several quite distinct types of fear: reflex avoidances, heart-in-the-mouth fearful reactions to situations perceived as dangerous, and generalized metaphysical anxieties about one's non-being" ("Fearing Death", *Philosophy* 58 (1983), 175–88; esp. 183). Animals can manifest the first and perhaps the second kinds of fear; but those in the third category are unique to human beings.

9. This implausible thesis is, however, proposed by Leming & Dickinson, *Understanding Dying*, 65.

10. It is worth pointing out that a failure to think (much) about death is not necessarily a result of deliberate evasion. Young people in particular may rarely think about death because it is not yet on their horizon. Does that make them inauthentic? It may be said in their defence that they are likely to have many more pressing things to do at their time of life than squaring up to death. Sufficient to the day are the evils thereof. Aristotle remarks in the *Rhetoric* that "we do not fear things that are a very long way off: for instance, we all know that we shall die, but we are not troubled thereby, because death is not close at hand" (1382a; *Rhetoric*, W. Rhys Roberts (trans.), reprinted in *The Basic Works of Aristotle*, Richard McKeon (ed.), 1325–451 [New York: The Modern Library, 2001], 1389). However, Aristotle seems rather oddly to forget that death is a lot closer at hand for the old than for the young.

11. Quoted in Ignace Lepp, *Death and its Mysteries* (London: Burns & Oates, 1969), 6.

12. Over the past thirty or so years there has been much debate over whether Western society as a whole has become death-denying. Ernest Becker's book *The Denial of Death* (New York: Free Press, 1973) contended that Americans could no longer bear to think or talk about death, which had become a taboo subject in polite society. Becker and others who thought like him were successful in sparking a widespread debate that, by the very fact of its occurrence, was strong evidence that the thesis was false. Michael Simpson remarked in 1979 that "Death is a very badly kept secret; such an unmentionable and taboo topic that there are over 750 books now in print asserting that we are ignoring the subject" (*Death, Dying and Grief: A Critical Bibliography* [New York: Plenum, 1979], preface; I am indebted for this reference to Sarah Tarlow, *Bereavement and Commemoration: An Archaeology of Mortality* [Oxford: Blackwell, 1999], 6). A quarter of a century later there are a great many more books on death (including the present one) and death studies are thriving in the academy. It is almost as if we are fearful of being fearful of death.

13. Aristotle's discussion of courage is to be found at *Nicomachean Ethics*, 1115b–1117b (D. Ross [trans.] [Oxford: Oxford University Press, 1954], 63–72).

14. Is someone who engages in a dangerous hobby such as rock-climbing or hang-

gliding, then, not brave? Do these activities not take guts? They do, but it would be hard to justify them if the risks taken were more than minimal. (It would be a perversion of bravery, or what Aristotle would term "recklessness", to play Russian roulette with a loaded pistol.) However, in so far as the desired payoff is the thrill of dicing with death, some question of their rationality may be raised, although we shall not pursue it here.

15. In Kipling's poem of the same name, the not-so-virtuous soldier Danny Deever is hanged by the regiment for shooting a sleeping comrade.

16. Steven Luper has devised the term "thanatizing" as a label for the intentional killing of those of one's desires that can be frustrated by death. Death is not a misfortune for those who have "thanatized" their aspirations ("thanatics") "because they do not care about living nor, ultimately, about anything for which living is necessary" (*Invulnerability*, 117–18). Luper regards this as an extremely foolish way of coming to terms with mortality, although it has been endorsed by some philosophers. Thanatics have "completely sabotaged their motivation for living" (*ibid*.: 141) and their lives are effectively living deaths.

17. I have changed Rouse's wording "practising dying" to "practising for dying", which more accurately captures Socrates' meaning. Philosophers are not practising dying as such but rather that activity that will be their sole concern after death. (It is not made clear, however, whether those who have honed their philosophical skills during life can expect to be better philosophers in the afterlife.)

18. It is interesting to note that Plato – or Socrates – may not be wholly committed to the view of the afterlife set out in the *Phaedo*. In his account of the trial of Socrates, Plato represents the older philosopher as offering a disjunctive analysis of death: *either* the dead are nothing and have no consciousness at all, *or* death is "a change and a migration for the soul from this place here to another place". If the former disjunct is true, then death would be like an untroubled, dreamless sleep, and hence a great blessing (*Apology*, 40c–d; in *Great Dialogues of Plato*, 445). As Socrates has just been unjustly condemned for death on charges of impiety and corruption of the young, he may be forgiven for the world-weariness conveyed in this upbeat judgement of non-existence.

19. Montaigne is referring to Cicero, *Tusculan Disputations*, I.xxx.74–xxxi.75.

20. Note that more recent editions of La Rochefoucauld are available, but I have preferred to quote him in the splendidly vigorous (although anonymous) eighteenth-century translation published for the Royal Society.

21. Elsewhere La Rochefoucauld writes that "Death and the sun are not to be looked at steadily" (François Duc de La Rochefoucauld [Prince of Marçillac], *Maxims and Moral Reflections of the Duke de la Rochefoucauld* [London: Lockyer Davis, 1786], 27).

22. One philosopher who was not was David Hume. He famously remarked that "Reason is, and ought only to be the slave of the passions, and can never pretend to any other office but to serve and obey them". See *A Treatise of Human Nature*, L. A. Selby-Bigge (ed.) (Oxford: Clarendon Press, 1888), bk. II. pt. III. § III; 415.

23. See, for instance, the Roman poet Horace, who aspired to leave behind a body of verse that would be *monumentum aere perennius*, a "monument more permanent than bronze" (*Odes*, bk. III. 30; *The Odes of Horace*, J. Michie [trans.] [Harmondsworth: Penguin, 1967]).

24. They could, of course, do a great deal of harm or good to human beings, as

Greek mythology amply demonstrates. This might provide them with their best opportunity for virtuous or vicious behaviour that exceeded the mediocre. In their relations with their equals, however, their scope for significantly virtuous or vicious action remains unsatisfactorily constricted.

25. Whether, as they also claim, this justifies God in having placed us in a setting as challenging as this one is perhaps rather more moot. When John Hick describes our world as a "vale of soul-making" he appears to forget that for many people who fall victim to its myriad natural and moral evils it is rather a vale of soul-breaking. See John Hick, *Evil and the God of Love*, 2nd edn (London: Macmillan, 1977), 253–61. (The phrase "vale of soul-making" is borrowed from a letter of John Keats to George and Georgiana Keats written in 1819.)

Chapter 5: The evil of death

1. Such a subject might be thought of as consisting in some kind of soul-material in a permanent state of sleep or coma. But we could have no reasonable ambition to "survive" in such a form, even if, as seems doubtful, the notion of such existence could be made metaphysically intelligible.

2. In a private communication, Luper has explained that he does not regard the absurdity of Epicurus's argument as a reason for ignoring it: "lots of patent falsehoods attract attention: scepticism, solipsism, etc.". But "a claim is absurd if it is so out of tune with a reasonable attitude to life". However, I personally prefer to call the argument "incredible" rather than "absurd".

3. The Epicurean argument has been sympathetically regarded by, for example, Stephen Rosenbaum, "Epicurus and Annihilation", reprinted in Fischer, *The Metaphysics of Death*, 293–304, and Stephen Hetherington, "Deathly Harm", *American Philosophical Quarterly* 38, (2001), 349–62 and "Lucretian Death: Asymmetries and Agency", *American Philosophical Quarterly* 42 (2005), 211–19.

4. Cf. Feldman's slightly reworded version of his anti-Epicurean argument in his *Confrontations with the Reaper: A Philosophical Study of the Nature and Value of Death* (Oxford: Oxford University Press, 1992), ch. 9.

5. The somewhat vague notion of "intrinsic badness" is characterized by Feldman as follows: "[I]f someone says that a state of affairs, p, is intrinsically bad for a person s, he presumably means that p is intrinsically bad, and s is the subject or 'recipient' of p" ("Some Puzzles About the Evil of Death", *Philosophical Review* 100 (1991), 205–27, esp. 213). (The substitution "extrinsically bad" for "overall bad" is made in *Confrontations with the Reaper*, 149.)

6. Milton's Belial, whom we encountered in Chapter 2, preferred a life of pain to non-existence, but I suspect that his might be a minority view. In any case, Belial had a project (albeit a bad, revengeful one) to give his life meaning. Without such a project to supply an interest in living, it is hard to see what else would make existence in severe pain tolerable.

7. I am indebted to the illuminating discussion of this passage in James Warren, *Facing Death: Epicurus and his Critics* (Oxford: Clarendon Press, 2004), 34–41.

8. This objection is also effective against Ben Bradley's "Improved Deprivation Account" of the evil of death in "When is Death Bad for the One who Dies?", *Noûs* 38 (2004), 1–28. Space forbids a discussion of Bradley's theory, which he is candid enough to admit falls foul of the Draper objection (*ibid.*: 23–4).

9. McMahan says that it might nevertheless be a "misfortune" for a person to fail to fulfil a heartfelt but wholly unrealistic desire, even though it would not evoke our pity ("Death and the Value of Life", in Fischer, *The Metaphysics of Death*, 233–66, esp. 256). But it is not clear that we would not, or should not, pity a misfortune just because it was of this kind. Alternatively we could side with Draper and deny that such a failure constitutes a misfortune. It is worth remarking in this connection that if theism is false, then those who wish it to be true, or who have desires premised on its truth (such as the desire for an after-life in paradise), wish for things that are wide of the mark. Perhaps we should distinguish between desires for the unreal and desires for the unrealistic and classify misconceived religious desires with the former. But in any case it does not seem inappropriate to include the non-fulfilment of religious desires in the category of personal misfortunes.

10. The Epicurean–Lucretian view that death is not an evil and should not be viewed as a deprivation is, however, in some tension with the further strand of Epicurean thought that our lives are incomplete and unsatisfactory until we have attained the state of *ataraxia* (tranquillity). It follows from this latter thesis that it is possible to die too soon. Moreover, as Warren observes, since *ataraxia* is impossible so long as one fears death, having a (reasonable) fear that one will die before one has achieved that fortunate state is sufficient to ensure that one will *not* attain it. It is unlikely that Epicureans can resolve these inconsistencies without making major adjustments to key doctrines. For a fuller discussion, see Warren, *Facing Death*, ch. 4.

11. For George Pitcher's similar view, see "The Misfortunes of the Dead", *American Philosophical Quarterly* 21 (1984), 183–8. Cf., too, David Furley, "Nothing to us?", in *The Norms of Nature*, M. Schofield & G. Striker (eds), 75–91 (Cambridge: Cambridge University Press, 1986). Martha Nussbaum is also sympathetic to the general line of reasoning, affirming that "Our fear of death is a fear that, *right now*, our hopes and projects are vain and empty" ("Mortal Immortals: Lucretius on Death and the Voice of Nature", *Philosophy and Phenomenological Research*, 50 [1989], 303–51, esp. 317). Steven Luper sums up the position crisply: "It is not the dead who are harmed, but rather the living" ("Death", *Stanford Encyclopaedia of Philosophy*, http://plato.stanford.edu/entries/death [accessed Oct. 2006].

12. Stephen Hetherington has argued, in connection with an analogous example to that of the ploughboy, that the Pitcher–Feinberg theory seems to imply that "being dead as such" is not bad for us ("Deathly Harm", 353–4). But this is an exaggerated way of stating the difficulty, since Pitcher and Feinberg could reasonably retort that on their view we are harmed by events that happen after our dying and that are harmful because we have died. Still, it gestures towards what we might describe as the "intuitional deficit" of their line.

13. For a similar objection see Julian Lamont, "A Solution to the Puzzle of When Death Harms its Victims", *Australasian Journal of Philosophy* 76 (1998), 198–212, esp. 202–4.

14. Warren, *Facing Death*, 49, records that there is evidence that Epicurus himself took this view.

15. For another statement of the argument see *On the Nature of the Universe*, bk. 3, lines 832–42 (R. E. Latham [trans.] [Harmondsworth: Penguin, 1951], 121). Strictly speaking, Lucretius should talk about our pre-*conception* rather than our

prenatal non-existence, since we exist from conception onwards, although the period between that and our birth is an experiential blank. But since the modern discussion has largely followed Lucretius's terminology, I shall do the same here. There is some justification for this in that while biological life begins at conception, we reasonably think of our biographical lives as starting at birth.

16. The symmetry argument became popular in antiquity beyond the confines of the Epicurean school. Thus we find a lively version of it in a private letter from Seneca: "Wouldn't you think a man a prize fool if he burst into tears because he didn't live a thousand years ago? A man is as much a fool for shedding tears because he isn't going to be alive a thousand years from now. There's no difference between the one and the other – you didn't exist and you won't exist – you've no concern with either" (letter 77 in *Letters from a Stoic*, 127). Montaigne echoes the Senecan argument in his essay "To Philosophize is to Learn How to Die" (in *The Complete Essays*, 102).

17. For a recent defence of the argument see Stephen E. Rosenbaum, "The Symmetry Argument: Lucretius Against the Fear of Death", *Philosophy and Phenomenological Research* 50 (1989), 353–73.

18. It is worth remarking that Nagel thinks the argument about origins "too sophisticated" to explain our insouciance about our prenatal non-existence (although this does not rule out that it could justify it). See Thomas Nagel, "Death", in *Mortal Questions*, 1–10 (Cambridge: Cambridge University Press, 1979), 8–9 n.3.

19. Frederik Kaufman, "Death and Deprivation; Or, Why Lucretius's Symmetry Argument Fails", *Australasian Journal of Philosophy* 74 (1996), 305–12 has been criticized by A. L. Brueckner and J. M. Fischer ("Being Born Earlier", *Australasian Journal of Philosophy* 76 (1998), 110–14) on the grounds that Kaufman offers an inadequate explanation of how a psychological account of personal identity might operate across possible worlds. But even if Kaufman is wrong to think that a person *could not* (given the psychological differences) have been identical with someone living a hundred years earlier, it is still true, as he claims, that it would be extremely hard for a person in a position like Jane's to identify imaginatively with the person who would have existed if her embryo had been implanted a hundred years earlier; this earlier person would seem "a complete stranger" to her.

20. Derek Parfit, *Reasons and Persons* (Oxford: Clarendon Press, 1984), part 2, "Rationality and Time", is the *locus classicus*. The psychology and rationality of our bias towards the future have been discussed by innumerable subsequent authors.

21. Note that it would be incorrect to say that we could have *no* impact of any kind on the past, since there may be things we could do that would have retrospective significance of the kind discussed by Pitcher and Feinberg.

22. Arguably, not all instances of our bias towards the future exhibit rationality. Parfit thinks that most people would prefer to have had a truly excruciating experience in the past than to be facing a lesser, though still painful, experience tomorrow (*Reasons and Persons*, 193–4). Since rational agents can be expected, other things being equal, to prefer a lesser pain to a greater one, this preference (assuming Parfit is right about it) may seem perverse. Yet we are never actually in a position of having to choose whether to suffer in the past or in the future and, since the past is causally closed, there is evidently no practical point in

worrying about a pain that has already happened. If we were able to change the past, then the preference in question would be harder to defend. But in that deeply counterfactual situation it might not be our preference anyway.

23. See Chapter 4, n.16.

24. Ben Bradley takes the same view in "When is Death Bad", 4–5.

25. This formulation is adapted from E. J. Lowe, *A Survey of Metaphysics* (Oxford: Oxford University Press, 2002), 238. The term "Cambridge change" is generally attributed to Peter Geach, who identified it as a theme of interest to certain Cambridge philosophers of the early 1900s. Inevitably, real changes have sometimes been christened "Oxford changes".

26. This point has been made by a number of writers, including David-Hillel Ruben, "A Puzzle about Posthumous Predication", *The Philosophical Review* 97 (1988), 211–36, esp. 232–3 and William Grey, "Epicurus and the Harm of Death", *Australasian Journal of Philosophy* 77 (1999), 358–64, esp. 361. It is also anticipated, although without the use of the expression "Cambridge change", in W. J. Waluchow, "Feinberg's Theory of 'Preposthumous' Harm", *Dialogue* 25 (1986), 727–34, esp. 734.

27. To undergo relational change a thing must at some stage have had some intrinsic properties, otherwise there would be nothing to individuate it or in virtue of which it could enter into relations with other things. The time that Tolstoy had such properties was when he was a living man.

28. Cf. Lowe, *A Survey of Metaphysics*, 238–9, for a discussion of the nature of change involved in becoming older.

Chapter 6: The interests of the dead

1. Wilkinson appears to want to attribute even such putative new interests that arise after death to the ante-mortem subject. But it seems very strained to ascribe to the living subject an interest that cannot exist contemporaneously with that subject.

2. See Dominic Scott, "Aristotle on Posthumous Fortune", *Oxford Studies in Ancient Philosophy* 18 (2000), 211–29, esp. 229. Presumably Aristotle understands the notion of surviving in one's handiwork in a metaphorical rather than a literal sense. There is some anthropological evidence of societies that consider people not as bounded individuals with alienable possessions but as relational bundles in which living persons and their possessions form some kind of whole. Taken literally, such conceptions would imply that there is survival of death in so far as parts of the person-constituting "bundle" survive. This would not, however, count as personal survival on *our* understanding of that notion, since for us it is an *a priori* postulate that people and their possessions are distinct existences. It is plausible to ascribe the same understanding to Aristotle.

3. Note that Nozick does not presume, as Browne appears to, that it is important to be personally remembered for the mark one makes. On Nozick's view, a life would have its value enhanced by making a valuable contribution to the human good even though the author of the contribution is never known or soon forgotten. But it is arguably better for the subject to make a contribution *and* be remembered for it.

4. The destruction of the temple (the "Artemision") is generally dated to 355 BCE.

5. It may be noted that one thing, A, can "subserve" another thing, B, in either of two different ways: A may be causally instrumental in bringing about B, or A may be a constitutive part or condition of B. For present purposes there is no need to labour the distinction.

6. The vanity of human life is a running theme in Leo Tolstoy's autobiographical work, *My Confession*. For handy extracts, see Oswald Hanfling (ed.), *Life and Meaning: A Reader* (Oxford: Blackwell, 1987), 9–19.

7. I say a little more about this issue in "On Caring about our Posthumous Reputation", *American Philosophical Quarterly* 38 (2001), 209–17, esp. 216–17.

Chapter 7: Dealing with the dead

1. Tim Mulgan contends that it behoves "liberal political philosophers" who are concerned to delineate the rights of the dead to be "suitably impartial concerning the ontological status of the dead" ("The Place of the Dead in Liberal Political Philosophy", *Journal of Political Philosophy* 7 (1999), 52–70, esp. 70). It is true that political philosophers, liberal or otherwise, should be sensitive to cultural differences when they debate such issues as the proper treatment of the dead or the demands made by some indigenous groups for the repatriation of their ancestors' remains from museum and private collections. But it would be unrealistic to suppose that a satisfactory account of our ethical relations with the dead could be devised that left in abeyance all the ontological questions. Although philosophers should not beg questions, they must often take stands.

2. "Act in such a way that you treat humanity, whether in your own person or in any other person, always at the same time as an end, and never merely as a means" (*Groundwork for the Metaphysics of Morals*, A. Zweig [trans.] [Oxford: Oxford University Press, 2002]), §2, 230).

3. Commenting on the same Shakespearean sonnet (although misnumbering it 77), Douglas J. Davies remarks that while many people nowadays have lost their personal fear of death and what comes after, they still care very much about the effect of their death on others (*A Brief History of Death* [Oxford: Blackwell, 2005], 97).

4. For the full text of the Vermillion Accord see www.worldarchaeologicalcongress. org/site/about_ethi.php (accessed October 2006).

5. The archaeologist Gerald Vizenor has proposed that human rights should be ascribed to bones, and that "bone courts" should be set up in which the rights of bones to be left in peace by researchers or developers would be asserted by trained advocates ("Bone Courts: The Rights and Narrative Representation of Tribal Bones", in *Contemporary Archaeology in Theory: A Reader*, I. Hodder & R. Preucel [eds], 652–63 [London: Routledge, 1996]). This proposal has not surprisingly been regarded as baroque by most of his professional colleagues. Once it is acknowledged that there can be moral obligations to dead people there is in fact no need to pursue Vizenor's strained notion that bones themselves possess human rights.

6. US Supreme Court, in *Planned Parenthood v. Casey*, 505 US 833, 851 (1992); quoted in Julian Baggini, "The Case for Legalised Euthanasia", *Philosopher's Magazine* 1 (1997), 26–31, esp. 27.

7. There *might* be a case for making an exception where those wishes were patently absurd or irrational, or where their fulfilment would lead to great harm

befalling the subject, or even his death. This is not the place to pursue this controversy, which is, of course, at the heart of the debate over whether voluntary active euthanasia should be legalized. In any case, Theseus's hypothesized grounds for not wanting his remains disturbed are perfectly reasonable ones. (Note that "reasonable" here does not imply "based on true assumptions". If Theseus wants to be left alone because he believes that disturbance will harm his spirit, while we may think the premise wrong it would be arrogant of us to dismiss as absurd a view that many reasonable human beings in other cultural traditions have upheld.)

8. A related argument, that archaeology serves the interests of the people under investigation by providing them with a history, has not gone unnoticed by the scholarly community. Thus the anthropologist Clement W. Meighan has written: "In my view, archaeologists have a responsibility to the people they study. They are defining the culture of an extinct group and in presenting their research they are writing a chapter of human history that cannot be written except from archaeological investigation. If the archaeology is not done, the ancient people remain without a history" ("Burying American Archaeology", in *Archaeological Ethics*, Karen D. Vitelli [ed.], 209–20 [Walnut Creek, CA: AltaMira Press, 1996], 210). It should, however, in fairness be noted that there has been much objection from some indigenous groups to archaeologists' pretensions to interpret their past history for them.

9. Kastenbaum suggests that the popular attribution of some special knowledge or wisdom to dying people may stem from a twentieth-century tendency to romanticize the dying person. However, it is not clear that this attribution is particularly new. The final words of the great (and sometimes of the not so great) have been thought worthy of record in all ages. King David and Socrates are prominent examples in antiquity. Closer to our own day, James Boswell rushed to the death-bed of David Hume in 1776 in the hope of hearing some memorable reflections on last things.

10. The popular literary motif of the death-bed confession, where the villain owns up to the crimes that he has carefully concealed during life, may well be a vestige of the Christian practice of the shriving of the dying.

11. "I've lived a life that's full./I've travelled each and every highway;/But more, much more, than this,/I did it my way" (*My Way*, lyric by Paul Anka, sung by Frank Sinatra, released by Warner Brothers, 1969). One may, of course, live a full and satisfying life without travelling down every highway. However, there can be individual but very narrow or eccentric life choices that seriously circumscribe the development of a person's potential. This is why it is something, but not everything, to have done it "my way".

Bibliography

This bibliography lists all titles mentioned in the text plus a selection of further useful reading.

Appiah, K. A. 2005. *The Ethics of Identity*. Princeton, NJ: Princeton University Press.

Aquinas, T. 1947. *Summa Theologica*, Fathers of the English Dominican Province (trans.), 3 vols. New York: Benziger Brothers.

Aristotle 1954. *Nicomachean Ethics*, D. Ross (trans.). Oxford: Oxford University Press.

Aristotle 2001a. *De Interpretatione*, E. M. Edghill (trans.). In *The Basic Works of Aristotle*, R. McKeown (ed.), 40–61. New York: The Modern Library.

Aristotle 2001b. *Rhetoric*, W. R. Roberts (trans.). In *The Basic Works of Aristotle*, R. McKeown (ed.), 1325–451. New York: The Modern Library.

Arneson, R. 1999. "What, if Anything, Renders all Humans Morally Equal?". In *Singer and His Critics*, D. Jamieson (ed.), 103–28. Oxford: Blackwell.

Augustine 1945. *The City of God*, J. Healey (trans.), 2 vols. London: Everyman's Library.

Ayau, E. H. 2002. "*Ka Huaka 'I O Na 'Ōiwi*: The Journey Home". In *The Dead and their Possessions: Repatriation in Principle, Policy and Practice*, C. Fforde, J. Hubert & P. Turnbull (eds), 171–89. London: Routledge.

Baggini, J. 1997. "The Case for Legalised Euthanasia". *Philosophers' Magazine* 1, 26–31.

Becker, E. 1973. *The Denial of Death*. New York: Free Press.

Belliotti, R. A. 1979. "Do Dead Human Beings have Rights?". *The Personalist* 60, 201–10.

Belshaw, C. 2000. "Death, Pain and Time". *Philosophical Studies* 97, 317–41.

Belshaw, C. 2005. *Good Questions about Life and Death*. Oxford: Blackwell.

Bigelow, J., J. Campbell & R. Pargetter 1990. "Death and Well-being". *Pacific Philosophical Quarterly* 71, 119–40.

Borges, J. L. 1970. "The Immortal". In *Labyrinths*, D. A. Yates & J. E. Irby (trans.). Harmondsworth: Penguin.

Boswell, J. 1949. *The Life of Samuel Johnson, LL.D*. London: Everyman's Library.

Bradley, B. 2004. "When is Death Bad for the One who Dies?" *Noûs* 38, 1–28.

Browne, T. 1969. "Christian Morals. In *Religio Medici and Other Writings*. London: Everyman's Library.

Brueckner, A. L. & J. M. Fischer 1993. "Why is Death Bad?". See Fischer (1993a), 221–9.

Brueckner, A. L. & J. M. Fischer 1998. "Being Born Earlier". *Australasian Journal of Philosophy* 76, 110–14.

Cave, P. & B. Larvor (eds) 2004. *Thinking about Death*. London: British Humanist Association.

Cicero 1945. *Tusculan Disputations*, 2nd ed., J. E. King (trans.). Cambridge, MA: Harvard University Press.

Cooper, A. A. (3rd Earl of Shaftesbury) 1727. *Characteristicks of Men, Manners, Opinions, Times*, 3 vols. London.

Cooper, D. E. 1999. *Existentialism: A Reconstruction*, 2nd ed. Oxford: Blackwell.

Cooper, D. E. 2003. *Meaning*. Chesham: Acumen.

Dalton, P. C. 1979–80. "Death and Evil". *The Philosophical Forum* 11, 193–211.

Dastur, F. 1996. *Death: An Essay on Finitude*, J. Llewelyn (trans.). London: Athlone.

Davidson, D 1995. "Laws and Causes". *Dialectica* 49, 263–79.

Davies, D. J. 2005. *A Brief History of Death*. Oxford: Blackwell.

de Beauvoir, S. 1969. *A Very Easy Death*, P. O'Brian (trans.). Harmondsworth: Penguin.

de Beauvoir, S. 1972. *Old Age*, P. O'Brian (trans.). London: André Deutsch/Weidenfeld & Nicolson.

Diogenes Laertius 1925. *The Lives of the Philosophers*, R. D. Hicks (trans.). London: Heinemann.

Donnelly, J. (ed.) 1978. *Language, Metaphysics, and Death*. New York: Fordham University Press.

Draper, K. 1999. "Disappointment, Sadness, and Death". *Philosophical Review* 108, 387–414.

Draper, K. 2004. "Epicurean Equanimity towards Death". *Philosophy and Phenomenological Research* 69, 92–114.

Dreyfus, H. & M. Wrathall (eds) 2005. *The Blackwell Companion to Heidegger*. Oxford: Blackwell.

Dworkin, R. 1993. *Life's Dominion*. New York: Knopf.

Edwards, J. 1788. *Practical Sermons Never Before Published*. Edinburgh: M. Gray.

Edwards, P. 1975. "Heidegger and Death as 'Possibility'". *Mind* 84, 548–66.

Edwards, P. (ed.) 1997. *Immortality*. Amherst, NY: Prometheus.

Elias, N. 1985. *The Loneliness of the Dying*, E. Jephcott (trans.). Oxford: Blackwell.

Epicurus 1926. *The Extant Fragments*, C. Bailey (ed.). Oxford: Clarendon Press.

Estienne, H. 1594. *Les Premices, ou le livre des proverbes epigrammatisez, ou des epigrammes proverbialez*. Geneva: H. Estienne.

Feifel, H. (ed.) 1959. *The Meaning of Death*. New York: McGraw-Hill.

Feinberg, J. 1984. *The Moral Limits of the Criminal Law. Volume One: Harm to Others*. Oxford: Oxford University Press.

Feldman, F. 1991. "Some Puzzles About the Evil of Death". *Philosophical Review* 100, 205–27.

Feldman, F. 1992. *Confrontations with the Reaper: A Philosophical Study of the Nature and Value of Death*. Oxford: Oxford University Press.

Fingarette, H. 1996. *Death: Philosophical Soundings*. Chicago, IL: Open Court.

Fischer, J. M. 2005. "Free Will, Death, and Immortality: The Role of Narrative". *Philosophical Papers* 34, 379–403.

Fischer, J. M. (ed.) 1993a. *The Metaphysics of Death*. Stanford, CA: Stanford University Press.

Fischer, J. M. 1993b. "Recent Work on Death and the Meaning of Life". *Philosophical Books* 34, 65–75.

Flecker, J. E. 1922. *Hassan*. London: Heinemann.

Freud, S. 1996. "Thoughts for the Times on War and Death". Excerpted in *Death: Philosophical Soundings*, H. Fingarette, 149–56. Chicago, IL: Open Court.

Fuchs, A. E. 1990–91. "Posthumous Satisfactions and the Concept of Individual Welfare". *Journal of Philosophical Research* 16, 345–51.

Furley, D. 1986. "Nothing to us?". In *The Norms of Nature*, M. Schofield & G. Striker (eds), 75–91. Cambridge: Cambridge University Press.

Gaita, R. 2004. *The Philosopher's Dog*. London: Routledge.

Gervais, K. G. 1986. *Redefining Death*. New Haven, CT: Yale University Press.

Glannon, W. 1993. "Epicureanism and Death". *The Monist* 76, 222–34.

Glover, J. 1977. *Causing Death and Saving Lives*. Harmondsworth: Penguin.

Grey, W. 1999. "Epicurus and the Harm of Death". *Australasian Journal of Philosophy* 77, 358–64.

Grover, D. 1987. "Death and Life". *Canadian Journal of Philosophy* 17, 711–32.

Grover, D. 1989. "Posthumous Harm". *Philosophical Quarterly* 39, 334–53.

Hanfling, O. (ed.) 1987. *Life and Meaning: A Reader*. Oxford: Blackwell.

Harsthorne, C. 1958. "Outlines of a Philosophy of Nature, Part 2". *The Personalist* 39, 380–91.

Heidegger, M. 1962. *Being and Time*, J. Macquarrie & E. Robinson (trans.). Oxford: Blackwell.

Hetherington, S. 2001. "Deathly Harm". *American Philosophical Quarterly* 38, 349–62.

Hetherington, S. 2005. "Lucretian Death: Asymmetries and Agency". *American Philosophical Quarterly* 42, 211–19.

Hick, J. 1977. *Evil and the God of Love*, 2nd ed. London: Macmillan.

Horace (Quintus Horatius Flaccus) 1967. *The Odes of Horace*, J. Michie (trans.) Harmondsworth: Penguin.

Housman, A. E. 1939. *The Collected Poems of A. E. Housman*. London: Jonathan Cape.

Hume, D. 1888. *A Treatise of Human Nature*, L. A. Selby-Bigge (ed.). Oxford: Clarendon Press.

Hume, D. 1963. "On the Immortality of the Soul". In *Hume on Religion*, selected by R. Wolheim (ed.), 263–70. London: Collins.

Ishiguro, K. 1989. *The Remains of the Day*. New York: Knopf.

Jaspers, K. 1970. *Philosophy*, volume 2, E. B. Ashton (trans.). Chicago, IL: University of Chicago Press.

Kamm, F. M. 1988. "Why is Death Bad and Worse than Pre-natal Non-existence?". *Pacific Philosophical Quarterly* 69, 161–4.

Kant, I. 1991. *The Metaphysics of Morals*, M. Gregor (trans.). Cambridge: Cambridge University Press.

Kant, I. 2002. *Groundwork for the Metaphysics of Morals*, A. Zweig (trans.) Oxford: Oxford University Press.

Kastenbaum, R. 1993. "Last Words". *The Monist* **76**, 270–90.

Kaufman, F. 1996. "Death and Deprivation; Or, Why Lucretius's Symmetry Argument Fails". *Australasian Journal of Philosophy* **74**, 305–12.

Kaufmann, W. 1963. *The Faith of a Heretic*. New York: Anchor.

Kenny, A. 1989. "Wittgenstein's Meaning of Life". *Times Higher Education Supplement*, 19 May.

Klemke, E. D. (ed.) 2000. *The Meaning of Life*. Oxford: Oxford University Press.

Kübler-Ross, E. 1989. *On Death and Dying*. London: Routledge.

Lamont, C. 1965. "Mistaken Attitudes towards Death". *Journal of Philosophy* **52**, 29–36.

Lamont, J. 1998. "A Solution to the Puzzle of When Death Harms its Victims". *Australasian Journal of Philosophy* **76**, 198–212.

Larkin, P. 2003. *Collected Poems*, A. Twaite (ed.). London: Faber.

La Rochefoucauld, F., Duc de (Prince of Marçillac) 1786. *Maxims and Moral Reflections of the Duke de la Rochefoucauld*. London: Lockyer Davis.

Leming, M. R. & G. E. Dickinson 2002. *Understanding Dying, Death, and Bereavement*, 5th ed. Fort Worth, TX: Harcourt.

Lepp, I. 1969. *Death and its Mysteries*. London: Burns & Oates.

Levenbook, B. B. 1983. "Harming Someone after his Death". *Ethics* **94**, 407–19.

Loptson, P. 1998. "The Antinomy of Death". In *Death and Philosophy*, J. Malpas & R. Solomon (eds), 135–51. London: Routledge.

Lowe, E. J. 2002. *A Survey of Metaphysics*. Oxford: Oxford University Press.

Lucian 1961. *Dialogues of the Dead*. In *Works*, M. D. Macleod (trans.), vol. 7. Cambridge, MA: Loeb Classical Library.

Lucretius. 1951. *The Nature of the Universe*, R. E. Latham (trans.). Harmondsworth: Penguin.

Luper, S. 1996. *Invulnerability*. Chicago, IL: Open Court.

Luper, S. 2004. "Posthumous Harm". *American Philosophical Quarterly* **41**, 63–72.

Luper-Foy, S. 1993. "Annihilation". See Fischer (1993a), 269–90.

Luper-Foy, S. 2002. "Death", *Stanford Encyclopaedia of Philosophy*, http://plato.stanford.edu/entries/death (accessed September 2006).

Lynott, M. J. & A. Wylie (eds) 1995. *Ethics in American Archaeology: Challenges for the 1990s*. Washington DC: Society for American Archaeology.

MacIntyre, A. 1985. *After Virtue*. London: Duckworth.

MacIntyre, A. 1999. *Dependent Rational Animals*. London: Duckworth.

McMahan, J. 1988. "The Evil of Death". *Ethics* **99**, 32–61.

McMahan, J. 1993. "Death and the Value of Life". See Fischer (1993a), 233–66.

McMahan, J. 2002. *The Ethics of Killing: Killing at the Margins of Life*. Oxford: Oxford University Press.

Malpas, J. &. R. Solomon (eds) 1998. *Death and Philosophy*. London: Routledge.

Marcus Aurelius 1964. *Meditations*, M. Staniforth (trans.). Harmondsworth: Penguin.

Matthews, G. B. 1979. "Life and Death as the Arrival and Departure of the Psyche". *American Philosophical Quarterly* **16**, 151–7.

Meighan, C. W. 1996. "Burying American Archaeology". In *Archaeological Ethics*, K. D. Vitelli (ed.), 209–20. Walnut Creek, CA: AltaMira Press.

Mitsis, P. 1988. *Epicurus's Ethical Theory: The Pleasures of Invulnerability*. Ithaca, NY: Cornell University Press.

Montaigne, M. de 1987. *The Complete Essays*, M. A. Screech (ed. and trans.). Harmondsworth: Penguin.

Mothersill, M. 1987. "Death". In *Life and Meaning: A Reader*, O. Hanfling (ed.), 83–92. Oxford: Blackwell.

Mulgan, T. 1999. "The Place of the Dead in Liberal Political Philosophy". *Journal of Political Philosophy* 7, 52–70.

Mulhall, S. 2005. *Routledge Philosophy Guidebook to Heidegger and Being and Time*, 2nd edn. London: Routledge.

Nagel, T. 1979a. *Mortal Questions*. Cambridge: Cambridge University Press.

Nagel, T. 1979b. "Death". In *Mortal Questions*, 1–10. Cambridge: Cambridge University Press.

Nagel, T. 1979c. "The Absurd" . In *Mortal Questions*, 11–23. Cambridge: Cambridge University Press.

Nagel, T. 1986. *The View from Nowhere*. Oxford: Oxford University Press.

Nagel, T. 1987. *What Does it All Mean?* Oxford: Oxford University Press.

Nielsen, K. 2000. "Death and the Meaning of Life". In *The Meaning of Life*, E. D. Klemke (ed.), 153–9. Oxford: Oxford University Press.

Nozick, R. 1981. *Philosophical Explanations*. Oxford: Clarendon Press.

Nussbaum, M. 1989. "Mortal Immortals: Lucretius on Death and the Voice of Nature". *Philosophy and Phenomenological Research* 50, 303–51.

Parfit, D. 1984. *Reasons and Persons*. Oxford: Clarendon Press.

Partridge, E. 1981. "Posthumous Interests and Posthumous Respect". *Ethics* 91, 243–64.

Phillips, D. Z. 1970. *Death and Immortality*. London: Macmillan.

Pitcher, G. 1984. "The Misfortunes of the Dead". *American Philosophical Quarterly* 21, 183–8.

Plato 1956a. *Apology*. In *Great Dialogues of Plato*, W. H. D. Rouse (trans.), 422–46. New York: New American Library.

Plato 1956b. *Phaedo*. In *Great Dialogues of Plato*, W. H. D. Rouse (trans.), 460–521. New York: New American Library.

Plato 1953. *Symposium*. In *The Dialogues of Plato*, B. Jowett (trans.), 4th edn, vol. 1, 503–55. Oxford: Clarendon Press.

Polt, R. 1999. *Heidegger: An Introduction*. London: UCL Press.

Potts, M. & W. D. Evans 2005. "Does it Matter that Organ Donors are not Dead? Ethical and Policy Implications". *Journal of Medical Ethics* 31, 406–9.

Riding In 2000. "Repatriation: A Pawnee's Perspective". In *Repatriation Reader: Who Owns American Indian Remains?*, D. A. Mihesuah (ed.), 106–20. Lincoln, NE: University of Nebraska Press.

Robinson, J. 1988. "Personal Identity and Survival". *Journal of Philosophy* 85, 319–28.

Rorty, A. 1983. "Fearing Death". *Philosophy* 58, 175–88.

Rosenbaum, S. E. 1986. "How to be Dead and not Care: A Defense of Epicurus". *American Philosophical Quarterly* 23, 217–25.

Rosenbaum, S. E. 1989. "The Symmetry Argument: Lucretius Against the Fear of Death". *Philosophy and Phenomenological Research* 50, 353–73.

Rosenbaum, S. E. 1993. "Epicurus and Annihilation". See Fischer (1993a), 293–304.

Rosenberg, J. E. 1983. *Thinking Clearly about Death*. Englewood Cliffs, NJ: Prentice-Hall.

Ruben D.-H. 1988. "A Puzzle about Posthumous Predication". *Philosophical Review* 97, 211–36.

Russell, B. 1946. *History of Western Philosophy*. London: Allen & Unwin.

Sartre, J.-P. 1966. *Being and Nothingness*, H. E. Barnes (trans.). New York: Washington Square Press.

Sartre, J.-P. 1982. *Huis Clos*, K. Black (trans.). In *Huis Clos and Other Plays*, 177–223. Harmondsworth: Penguin.

Scarre, G. 1997. "Should We Fear Death?". *European Journal of Philosophy* 5, 269–82.

Scarre, G. 2001. "On Caring about our Posthumous Reputation". *American Philosophical Quarterly* 38, 209–17.

Scarre, G. 2006. "Can Archaeology Harm the Dead?". In *The Ethics of Archaeology: Philosophical Perspectives on Archaeological Practice*, C. Scarre & G. Scarre, (eds), 181–98. Cambridge: Cambridge University Press.

Scarre, C. & G. Scarre (eds) 2006. *The Ethics of Archaeology: Philosophical Perspectives on Archaeological Practice*. Cambridge: Cambridge University Press.

Scott, D. 2000. "Aristotle on Posthumous Fortune". *Oxford Studies in Ancient Philosophy* 18, 211–29.

Seale, C. 1998. *Constructing Death: the Sociology of Dying and Bereavement*. Cambridge: Cambridge University Press.

Secomb, L. 1999. "Philosophical Deaths and Feminine Fortitude". *Mortality* 4, 111–25.

Seneca 1969. *Letters from a Stoic*, selected by R. Campbell (trans.). Harmondsworth: Penguin.

Seneca 2005. *On the Shortness of Life*. In *Dialogues and Letters*, C. D. N. Costa (ed. and trans.), 59–83. Harmondsworth: Penguin.

Shewmon, D. A. 1998. "'Brain-stem Death', 'Brain-death' and Death: A Critical Reevaluation of the Purported Equivalence". *Issues in Law and Medicine* 14, 125–45.

Silverstein, H. 1980. "The Evil of Death". *Journal of Philosophy* 77, 401–20.

Simpson, M. 1979. *Death, Dying and Grief: A Critical Bibliography*. New York: Plenum.

Smith, A. 1976. *The Theory of Moral Sentiments*. In *The Glasgow Edition of the Works and Correspondence of Adam Smith*, D. D. Raphael & A. L. Macfie (eds), vol. 1. Oxford: Clarendon Press.

Solomon, R. 1998. "Death Fetishism, Morbid Solipsism". In *Death and Philosophy*, J. Malpas &. R. Solomon (eds), 152–76. London: Routledge.

Strawson, P. F. 1959. *Individuals*. London: Methuen.

Sumner, L. W. 1976. "A Matter of Life and Death". *Noûs* 10, 145–71.

Tarlow, S. 2006. "Archaeological Ethics and the People of the Past". In *The Ethics of Archaeology: Philosophical Perspectives on Archaeological Practice*, C. Scarre & G. Scarre (eds), 199–216. Cambridge: Cambridge University Press.

Tarlow, S. 1999. *Bereavement and Commemoration: An Archaeology of Mortality*. Oxford: Blackwell.

Taylor, R. 1984. *Good and Evil: A New Direction: A Forceful Attack on the Rationalistic Tradition in Ethics*. Buffalo, NY: Prometheus.

Thomas, D. 1993. *Collected Poems, 1934–1953*, W. Davies & R. Maud (eds). London: Dent.

Tolstoy, L. 1960. "The Death of Ivan Ilych". In *The Death of Ivan Ilych and Other Stories*, A. Maude *et al.* (eds), 95–126. New York: New American Library.

Tolstoy, L. 1987. *My Confession*. Excerpted in *Life and Meaning: A Reader*, O. Hanfling (ed.), 9–19. Oxford: Blackwell.

Unamuno, M. de [1912] 1931. *The Tragic Sense of Life in Men and in Peoples*, J. E. Crawford Flitch (trans.). London: Macmillan.

Valerius Maximus 1998. *Factorum et Dictorum Memorabilium Libri Novem [Nine Books of Memorable Deeds and Sayings]*, J. Briscoe (ed.). Stuttgart: Teubner

Van Evra, J. 1971. "On Death as a Limit". *Analysis* 31, 170–76.

Velleman, J. D. 2003. "Narrative Explanation". *Philosophical Review* 112, 1–26.

Velleman, J. D. 1993. "Well-being and Time". In *The Metaphysics of Death*, J. M Fischer (ed.), 329–57. Stanford, CA: Stanford University Press.

Vizenor, G. 1996. "Bone Courts: The Rights and Narrative Representation of Tribal Bones". In *Contemporary Archaeology in Theory: A Reader*, I. Hodder & R. Preucel (eds), 652–63. London: Routledge.

Wagner, R. 1965. *Tristan und Isolde*, S. Robb (trans.). New York: G. Schirmer.

Waluchow, W. J. 1986. "Feinberg's Theory of 'Preposthumous' Harm". *Dialogue* 25, 727–34.

Warren, J. 2004. *Facing Death: Epicurus and His Critics*. Oxford: Clarendon Press.

Wilkinson, T. M. 2002. "Last Rights: The Ethics of Research on the Dead [1]". *Journal of Applied Philosophy* 19, 31–41.

Williams, B. 1973a. *Problems of the Self*. Cambridge: Cambridge University Press.

Williams, B. 1973b. "The Makropulos Case: Reflections on the Tedium of Immortality". In *Problems of the Self*, 82–100. Cambridge: Cambridge University Press.

Williams, B. 1973c. "The Self and the Future". In *Problems of the Self*, 46–63. Cambridge: Cambridge University Press.

Wittgenstein, L. 1969. *Tractatus Logico-Philosophicus*, D. F. Pears & B. F. McGuiness (trans.). London: Routledge & Kegan Paul.

Wreen, M. J. 1987. "The Definition of Death". *Public Affairs Quarterly* 1, 87–99.

Yourgrau, P. 1987. "The Dead". *Journal of Philosophy* 84, 84–101.

Index